Uniforms of the

Napoleonic Wars

in colour

1796—1814

Devised and Illustrated by
JACK CASSIN-SCOTT

Military Research by
JOHN FABB

Text by
PHILIP J. HAYTHORNTHWAITE

BLANDFORD PRESS · POOLE

First published in the UK 1973 by Blandford Press Ltd.,
Link House, West Street, Poole, Dorset BH15 1LL.
Reprinted 1977 and 1985

Distributed in the United States by
Sterling Publishing Co., Inc.,
2 Park Avenue, New York, NY 10016.

ISBN 0 7137 1662 2

Printed in Spain by Graficromo

CONTENTS

HISTORICAL INTRODUCTION

The French Revolutionary and Napoleonic Wars
1792–1814

Encouraged by exiled French aristocrats, and fearful of the spread of the revolutionary ideas which had caused the overthrow of the Ancien Régime in France, Prussia and Austria declared themselves ready in 1792 to lead all other European powers in a campaign to restore the French monarchy. In April 1792 France seized the initiative by declaring war on Austria, and in August an Allied army of Prussians, Austrians, Hessians and French émigrés numbering 80,000 invaded France. The French army, an odd mixture of regulars, volunteers and National Guard managed to repel this force at Valmy (20 September). An outnumbered Austrian contingent was defeated at Jemappes and Brussels was captured by the French in November.

King Louis XVI was executed on 21 January 1793, and France declared war on England, Holland and Spain. France was invaded, and the French army defeated at Valenciennes, the commander, General Custine, being guillotined by his own government as a punishment! By August France was being attacked by Austrian, Prussian, Dutch and Anglo-Hanoverian armies, and torn by internal monarchist counter-revolutions. On 23 August the entire male population of France was conscripted on the 'levée en masse', and sheer weight of numbers, coupled with the patriotic zeal of the Revolution, and the organisational ability of War Minister Carnot, brought about a French revival, which by December had driven the invaders across the Rhine. An Anglo-Spanish expedition to Toulon in support of a monarchist revolt was defeated thanks to an obscure Corsican artillery officer, one Napoleon Bonaparte.

The year 1794 saw further French victories, notably at Fleurus (26 June), which led to the abandonment of Belgium by the Austrians; General Moreau laid siege to Mainz, Holland was invaded, and the Allies were driven out of Savoy. The only Allied success of the year was that of the 'Glorious First of June', when Britain's Lord Howe defeated a French naval squadron in the Atlantic, sinking one and capturing six French ships. In 1795 Holland became the satellite Batavian Republic, and Prussia, Saxony, Spain, Hanover and Hesse–Cassel made peace with France. In August the French National Convention, which had governed France since the Revolution, was dissolved, being replaced by a five-man 'Directory'. A monarchist outbreak in Paris was suppressed by General Bonaparte. The year ended with another French setback on the Rhine.

The Italian Campaigns 1796–98

Lazare Carnot – now effectively Chief of Staff as well as Minister of War – planned to defeat the Allies by a 'pincer' movement, one army advancing through Germany, and one through Italy, to unite at Vienna. The war had changed its character from a defence of her territory to a war of conquest by France, the motivation originally being the spread of revolutionary doctrine. In 1796 two French armies invaded Germany, but both were repelled by the capable Archduke Charles of Austria. In Italy, however, France was more successful. General Bonaparte, in command of the wretchedly equipped army of Italy, was opposed by an Austrian and a Piedmontese army. Driving between the Allied forces, Bonaparte defeated the Piedmontese at Mondovi (21 April), turned on the Austrians, defeated them at Lodi (10 May) and entered Milan. Eleven days later, Piedmont made peace, surrendering Savoy and Nice to France. The brilliance of the new French general was becoming evident.

Pursuing the Austrians, Bonaparte laid siege to Mantua; by the beginning of June it was the only part of northern Italy not in French hands. Two Austrian armies marched to its relief, and again Bonaparte split them apart and defeated them in detail, at Lonato and Castiglione, renewing the siege of Mantua in August. In September Bonaparte defeated two more Austrian forces, at Caliano and Bassano, and Mantua, though a relief column had reached it, remained under siege. In November, a third attempt to relieve the city was defeated at Arcola.

In January 1797 another attempt at the relief of Mantua was defeated at Rivoli, and on 2 February the 16,000 Austrian troops in Mantua capitulated. After receiving reinforcements from France, Bonaparte invaded Austria in March, employing the now-familiar tactic of separating the enemy forces by striking between them. The Austrians, now commanded by Archduke Charles, fell back before the French, until Bonaparte was only ninety-five miles from Vienna. This coinciding with a new French offensive on the Rhine, Austria sued for peace; Bonaparte dictated the truce terms without reference to the Directory, and these were confirmed by the Treaty of Campo Formio (17 October 1797), by which Belgium became part of France, and a French satellite state in northern Italy, the Cisalpine Republic, was recognised by Austria. Though the revolutionary fervour of the French people and the genius of Carnot undoubtedly were important factors, the main credit for the successful conclusion of the war must go to the strategic and tactical skill of young Bonaparte, who baffled and outmanoeuvred his more pedestrian opponents. The only Allied successes of 1797 were those of the British navy, at Cape St. Vincent (14 February) when Admiral Jervis defeated the Spanish fleet (Spain having allied with France in August 1796) and at Camperdown (11 October) when Admiral Duncan defeated the Dutch fleet.

The Expedition to Egypt

In February 1798 Rome was occupied, the Pope captured, and a Roman Republic proclaimed, and in April Switzerland was occupied, and a Helvetian Republic established. Bonaparte was put in command of the 'Army of England' assembled at Dunkirk for a proposed invasion. Discouraged by the British dominance of the seas, Bonaparte persuaded the Directory to launch an expedition to Egypt, which would provide a base from which the British could be expelled from India.

The politicians, anxious to remove the potential threat to themselves from a popular, successful leader, in April gave Bonaparte his Army of the Orient. The expedition sailed from Toulon and landed at Alexandria in July, having captured Malta *en route*. The Egyptian army, largely composed of Mamelukes, who were courageous horsemen but totally unaccustomed to modern warfare, met Bonaparte on 21 July 1798 at the Battle of the Pyramids, and were heavily defeated. Cairo was captured, but on 1 August the French fleet, anchored in Aboukir Bay, was almost totally destroyed by Horatio Nelson's British Mediterranean fleet in the Battle of the Nile, thus isolating Bonaparte's army. Acre, its garrison commanded by Sir Sidney Smith, a British naval captain, withstood a French siege, and though Bonaparte defeated a Turkish relieving force at the Battle of Mount Tabor, plague broke out in the French camp and compelled a retreat. On 25 July, however, Bonaparte annihilated a Turkish force at the Battle of Aboukir, and stabilised the situation. Realising that further conquest was impossible without reinforcements, and alarmed at the situation in Europe, Bonaparte left the army and returned to France.

While Bonaparte was in Egypt, the French had suffered several reverses in Europe. In August, a French invasion of Ireland had failed, and in December Czar Paul I organised the Second Coalition, of Russia, Britain, Austria, Portugal, Naples and the Ottoman Empire. The plan was for a three-pronged attack on France from an Anglo-Russian army in the Netherlands, an Austrian army in Germany and an Austro-Russian-Neapolitan army in Italy. Though Naples dropped out of the Coalition by January 1799, the Russian Marshal Suvarov's Allied army inflicted repeated defeats on the French, so that by the end of the year almost all Bonaparte's gains of 1796–97 had been erased. In Germany, a French invasion under General Jourdan was checked by the Archduke Charles; in the Netherlands, the Duke of York's Anglo-Russian army met with partial success, but withdrew. In Switzerland, the French General Masséna's offensive was initially repulsed, though in September he inflicted a severe defeat on an Allied army at Zürich, and turned back Suvarov's advance from Italy. The campaigns of 1799 had been disappointing to both sides; the French had lost Italy, and the Allies had failed elsewhere. Russia withdrew from the Coalition in disgust.

The Marengo Campaign

The failures of 1799 paved the way for Bonaparte's *coup d'état* of 9 November, when he established a governmental system controlled by three Consuls, with himself as virtual dictator as First Consul. His offer of peace to the Allies was rejected, and Bonaparte took the field in Italy. By April 1800, Masséna was driven into Genoa and besieged, capitulating to the Austrians in June; but the arrival of the First Consul threw the Austrians on the defensive. On 14 June, the French and Austrians ran into each other at Marengo. With only 18,000 men against the 34,000 of the Austrian general Melas, Bonaparte fared badly, and was driven back two miles. Melas, thinking the battle won, advanced at a leisurely pace. Bonaparte, however, reinforced by General Desaix's corps, counter-attacked, the decisive blow being struck by Kellermann's French cavalry. The Austrian army was shattered and collapsed; the French success was complete, though the victory was as much a matter of good luck as anything else. Desaix was killed in the counter-attack. On the following day, the campaign virtually ended when Melas asked for an armistice, and Bonaparte returned to Paris.

In December 1800, General Moreau, advancing into Germany, crushed an Austrian army at Hohenlinden; General Macdonald invaded the Tirol with another French army, and on 25 December Austria sued for peace, the war ending by the Treaty of Lunéville in February 1801. In Egypt, however, the French had been less successful. Bonaparte's successor, Kléber, was assassinated on the day of Marengo, and in March 1801 a British expeditionary force defeated the French army at Aboukir. In August the French commander, Menou, capitulated, and Bonaparte's dream of oriental conquest was destroyed.

Following the Treaty of Lunéville, Russia, Prussia, Denmark and Sweden joined together in a league of 'Armed Neutrality' to protect their shipping against possible interference from Britain. British reaction was immediate; the fleet of Sir Hyde Parker sailed into Copenhagen harbour, where Horatio Nelson, Parker's second in command, destroyed Danish resistance in a five-hour battle (2 April 1801). Hostilities ended in June. In July Sir James Saumarez's British fleet gained a victory over a Franco-Spanish fleet near Gibraltar.

Napoleon, Emperor of the French

In March 1802 the Treaty of Amiens between Britain and France brought temporary peace to Europe, and on 2 August Bonaparte was proclaimed First Consul for life. This was a milestone in his life; in six years he had risen from an unknown artillery officer to the dictator of one of the most powerful states in Europe, gaining a formidable reputation as a brilliant and, compared to the rigid tactical theories of the late eighteenth century, unorthodox commander. The ragged, undisciplined masses of the revolutionary armies had been moulded into a professional, experienced and well-equipped army; the next ten years were to enhance Bonaparte's reputation to the point of legend. On 2 December 1804, Bonaparte was crowned as Napoleon, Emperor of the French.

Peace was short-lived; in May 1803 Britain imposed a naval blockade on the Continent, and Napoleon began preparations for the invasion of England. Britain responded to the threat of invasion by the raising of a volunteer force totalling over 400,000, and unprecedented patriotic movement. The volunteers, however, had never to face a French invasion, due to the complete superiority of the British navy which made a Channel crossing almost impossible, and in October 1804 the invasion flotilla was severely damaged by a British attack. Britain had no longer to face the French threat alone – she recruited Austria, Russia and Sweden into the Third Coalition. The Allies planned to take advantage of the French troop concentration at Boulogne by smashing Masséna's army in northern Italy before he could be reinforced, and then advancing on France.

In August 1805 Napoleon took the initiative, marching eastward from Boulogne. An Austrian army advanced towards him, but unaware of the French position. By a masterly outflanking movement, Napoleon manoeuvred his army behind that of the Austrian general Mack, who after a futile attempt to break the encirclement, was forced to surrender, at Ulm on 17 October. Ulm was not a battle, but a strategic victory which emphasised the brilliance of the French Emperor. On 30 October Masséna repelled the Austrian advance in Italy, and in the first two weeks of

November, Napoleon invaded Austria and occupied Vienna, driving the Russian army of Kutuzov before him. Napoleon continued to advance, putting his army into a position of apparent danger between two Allied armies, 18,000 men under the command of the Austrian Archduke Ferdinand, and 90,000 nominally under the Emperor Francis II of Austria and Czar Alexander I, though actually commanded by Kutuzov. A further 80,000 were prevented from crossing the Alps by the corps of Marshal Ney and General Marmont, and withdrew to Austria through Hungary south of the Alps. Kutuzov planned to circle the French army and cut its communications with Vienna, which was exactly what Napoleon had anticipated.

Austerlitz

Napoleon placed his army near the village of Austerlitz, deliberately presenting a weak right flank for the Allies to attack. On 2 December 1805, the Allied army hit this exposed flank and drove it back, a third of the army being concentrated on crushing the French right, and thus manoeuvring between the remainder of the French army and Vienna. Then Napoleon sprang his trap; the corps of Marshal Soult split the allied centre, encircled the left wing, and, assisted by the corps of Marshal Davout, drove it from the field. The Allied right wing, assaulted by the corps of Marshals Bernadotte and Lannes, resisted bravely, but by nightfall the Allied army was annihilated, losing 26,000 men to the French 9,000. Austerlitz was a tactical masterpiece of the highest order, and two days later forced an unconditional surrender by Austria. With the remnants of the Czar's army withdrawing to Russia, Napoleon had domination over western and southern Germany. His master-stroke of Austerlitz had changed the face of Europe.

Napoleon had suspended his projected invasion of England to embark on the Austerlitz campaign, and the destruction of the Franco-Spanish fleet at Trafalgar (21 October 1805) by Lord Nelson left Britain with undisputed mastery of the sea by the most decisive naval victory in history, though at the cost of Nelson's life.

The Defeat of Prussia

In 1806 Napoleon controlled central and western Germany by the formation of the Confederation of the Rhine, a political and military alliance of French satellite states. Prussia and Saxony, alarmed at French power, and encouraged by Britain, prepared for war. Napoleon, moving with amazing rapidity, invaded Prussia in October 1806. Detaching Marshals Davout and Bernadotte to cut the communications of the Duke of Brunswick's Prussian army, Napoleon advanced towards Jena. On 14 October Brunswick split his forces into two detachments, personally attacking Davout at Auerstadt. Napoleon struck the second Prussian force at Jena, and by noon had driven them from the field in confusion. Davout withstood Brunswick's attack at Auerstadt, then counter-attacked; Brunswick was killed, King Frederick William III assuming command, and when Bernadotte approached the Prussian rear, Frederick's army disintegrated, losing 50,000 in killed, wounded and prisoners; French losses were about 8,000 on both fields. Once again, by rapid movement and strategic genius, Napoleon had won a campaign at one blow; by the end of November all Prussian resistance had ceased, and Frederick William fled to Russia.

In January 1807 a Russian advance regained some of the Prussian territory, but on 8 February Napoleon counter-attacked at Eylau. Fought in a driving snowstorm, the battle was fought to a standstill with enormous casualties on both sides, and both armies withdrew to winter quarters. In June the Russo-Prussian offensive was resumed; Napoleon placed his army between the two Allied forces, and defeated Bennigsen's Russians at Friedland on 14 June. In July 1807, Napoleon met Frederick William of Prussia and Czar Alexander on a raft in the middle of the River Niemen, where the Treaties of Tilsit were signed. A French satellite, the Grand Duchy of Warsaw, was established, and Prussia relinquished to France and the Confederation of the Rhine all her territory between the Elbe and the Rhine, and payed an indemnity of 140,000,000 francs. Russia was compelled into an anti-British alliance with the French. Napoleon was master of western and central Europe.

The Peninsular War 1807–9

After Tilsit, Britain alone remained in opposition to Napoleon, maintaining a naval blockade of the entire coastline of Europe. In November 1806 Napoleon had imposed a counter-blockade by his Continental System; and after Tilsit the only opening to British trade was neutral Portugal. In an attempt to cut off this last access, Napoleon's general Junot led an army through Spain (with her permission) and captured Lisbon on 1 December 1807. On 17 December Napoleon announced the Milan Decrees, reaffirming the Continental System by forbidding all British trade from Europe (though in fact smuggling flourished!).

In June 1806 a small British force raided the Calabrian coast in support of guerrillas resisting Napoleon's brother Joseph, King of Naples, defeating a French army at Maida (4 July), after which the British withdrew to Sicily. In September 1807, fearing Denmark would join the Franco-Russian alliance, a British expedition was sent to Copenhagen. The Danish fleet was captured, and the city bombarded by a British landing party under the command of Sir Arthur Wellesley, a young general of great skill who had won fame in India.

In March 1808 Marshal Murat led 100,000 French troops into Spain under the pretext of guarding the Spanish coastline. The Spanish King was forced to abdicate, and Napoleon's brother Joseph crowned King of Spain. Insurrection followed, and grew into the bitter guerrilla war which was waged without quarter for the next six years. Spanish resistance was stimulated by the surrender of 20,000 French troops at Baylen in July; promise of safe conduct home was violated by the Spanish, those French who were not murdered being consigned into prison hulks where most died of disease and neglect. In August, a British expedition landed in Portugal under the command of Sir Arthur Wellesley. He defeated Junot at Vimiero (21 August) but was relieved of command when British generals of greater seniority arrived. Junot capitulated, his army being evacuated to France by the British navy. Outraged by this agreement, the British government recalled Wellesley and his superiors for an inquiry, in which Wellesley was vindicated of all blame. Meanwhile, the British army of Sir John Moore advanced into Spain, but was forced to retire when Napoleon himself assumed command of the French. Moore conducted a skilful but arduous retreat to Corunna, from where the army was evacuated after a hard-fought action on 16 January 1809, in which Moore was killed. The Spanish stronghold of Saragossa was captured by Marshal Lannes in February 1809, and Spain seemed under control.

Wagram

Napoleon left Spain when it became evident that Austria was preparing for war again. When Napoleon arrived in Germany in April 1809, he found the French army on the verge of defeat. In a week of brilliant manoeuvring, Napoleon defeated the Austrians four times, at Abensburg (19–20 April), Landeshut (21 April), Eggmühl (22 April) and Ratisbon (23 April), and on 13 May Vienna was captured. Continuing his pursuit of the Austrian army, Napoleon tried to cross the Danube, but his attack was repulsed at the Battle of Aspern-Essling (21–22 May). It was Napoleon's first defeat, and cost the life of Marshal Lannes. In July Napoleon crossed the Danube, and once again split his enemies, the Archduke Charles with 140,000 men, and Archduke John with 50,000. On 5–6 July, Napoleon attacked Charles at Wagram. On the second day of the battle, the Austrian centre was pierced, and Marshal Davout turned the left flank; Charles withdrew in good order, but with a loss of 45,000 men. On 10 July Austria asked for peace, as further resistance was hopeless; Austrian troops had been driven from the Grand Duchy of Warsaw by Prince Poniatowski's Polish army, and a British expedition to Walcheren in the Netherlands had failed, and no assistance had come from Russia. The Treaty of Schönnbrun (14 October) reaffirmed Napoleon's mastery of Europe.

The Peninsular War, 1809–12

In Spain, however, the guerrilla war continued with increasing brutality on both sides, and Wellesley had returned to Portugal with 26,000 British and Hanoverian troops, where he reorganised the Portuguese army under General Beresford. In March 1809 Marshal Soult invaded Portugal, but was defeated by Wellesley at Oporto (12 May). In June Wellesley took the offensive, and invaded Spain, supported by a Spanish army of little value. On 28 June a hard-fought battle at Talavera forced a French retreat, but when the Spanish general Cuesta withdrew his support, Wellesley returned to Portugal, and soon after was created Viscount Wellington. In November 1809 the Spanish army was smashed at Ocana. Wellington built a formidable defensive line north of Lisbon, at Torres Vedras, and waited for the French attack, which came in July 1810. Defeating the French at Busaco (27 September), Wellington withdrew behind the impregnable Torres Vedras lines, and Marshal Masséna's army was forced by lack of supplies to retire in November 1810.

Wellington's army was supplied easily through Lisbon, thanks to the dominance of the British navy; but the French, with long lines of communication, were forced to forage in a hostile land, under continual harrassment by guerrilla bands. The drain on manpower and resources caused by the war in the Iberian Peninsula was one of the principal factors which resulted in the downfall of Napoleon, consuming as it did much of the strength needed elsewhere; Napoleon termed the campaign his 'Spanish ulcer'.

In 1811 Soult and Masséna advanced on Portugal again. On 5 May Masséna was checked by Wellington at Fuentes de Oñoro, and on 16 May Soult was defeated by Beresford at Albuhera, in a battle of appalling carnage. The Spanish fled the field, but the extraordinary courage of the

British infantry saved the day and turned the tide of victory against the French, though at a terrible price. Masséna was replaced by Marshal Marmont, and for the remainder of the year the only conclusive operations were those of Marshal Suchet, who fought a successful campaign against the guerrillas in southern Spain.

In 1812 Wellington stormed the border fortresses of Ciudad Rodrigo and Badajos, and rapidly advanced into Spain. On 22 July in one of his greatest victories, he completely defeated Marmont at Salamanca, and followed the victory by the capture of Madrid in August. In November, however, a repulse at Burgos forced Wellington to retreat to Ciudad Rodrigo, an arduous withdrawal which cost 7,000 men. But the French armies of Soult and Marmont were unable to exist in the inhospitable countryside, and were compelled to disperse, giving the Allies time to recuperate.

The Invasion of Russia

In Europe, Franco-Russian relations steadily worsened. Encouraged by Britain, who made peace with Sweden and Russia in June 1812, both nations renounced the Continental System. In an attempt to recover from this serious economic blow, Napoleon planned an invasion of Russia from his base in Poland. His right protected by the Austrian army of Prince Schwarzenburg, and his left by a Franco-Prussian army under Marshal Macdonald, Napoleon intended to invade Russia with three armies, the principal one under his own command, supported by one under his stepson, Eugène de Beauharnais, and one under his brother Jérôme. This 'Grande Armée' of almost 510,000 contained less than half French, the remainder being an odd assortment of Germans, Polish, Italians and various other Europeans, many of dubious loyalty. He was opposed by three Russian armies.

Crossing the Niemen in June 1812, Napoleon planned to divide the two main Russian armies and defeat them in succession. The incompetent Jérôme, however, allowed the Russians to escape, and was replaced by Davout. Withdrawing before Napoleon, the Russian armies united at Smolensk, and fought a rearguard action. On 29 August Kutuzov assumed command of the combined Russian force, and drew the French on, stretching their lines of communication to the limit. On 7 September Kutuzov made a stand at Borodino. Napoleon attacked with slightly more than Kutuzov's 120,000 men, but unaccountably relinquished personal direction of the battle, the first of recurrent lapses, never fully explained medically, which hampered subsequent campaigns. After a day of almost indescribable carnage, the Russians recommenced their retreat, having lost 45,000 men to the French 35,000. The effect of this battle on the already exhausted French army, however, was decisive. On 14 September Napoleon entered Moscow, which was partly destroyed by Russian incendiaries. The exhausted Grande Armée, unable to live off the land, ran short of supplies, and on 19 October Napoleon decided to withdraw to Smolensk. He attacked Kutuzov at Maloyaroslavets, but was repulsed, and, as winter closed in, the retreat began. The commissariat having broken down, the starving French army was continually harrassed by swarms of irregular Cossacks who prevented the foraging for supplies, and repeated Russian attacks were beaten off. The allied troops became unreliable, and when Napoleon decided to continue the retreat from Smolensk (12 November), much of the army was a disorganised mob, an easy prey for the surrounding Cossacks. On 16 November the path of retreat was cut off by Kutuzov, who had circled west and barred the road at Krasnoi. Napoleon collected what effective troops he could and cleared the way, and the following day the 9,000 survivors of Marshal Ney's corps fought a desperate rearguard action from which only 800 returned. The Grande Armée limped to the River Beresina, which was crossed on 26–8 November. Attacking on both sides, the Russians were held off long enough for much of the French army to cross, but when the bridges were blown up thousands of stragglers were left on the east bank; they were either captured or massacred by the Cossacks. On 8 December Napoleon left for Paris, as the Grande Armée had ceased to exist; on 14 December Ney led the rearguard over the frontier at Kovno, and the campaign ended. Of the 450,000 of the central body of the Grande Armée, there were scarcely 1,000 effectives and a horde of stragglers left. The French lost over 300,000 of the campaign, the Russians 250,000. It was the beginning of the end for the French Emperor.

The Campaign of 1813

In January 1813 the Prussian and Austrian contingents of the Grande Armée defected, the Prussians joining the Russians, and the remainder of Prussia rose in rebellion. A new Coalition was formed of Britain, Russia, Prussia and Sweden. Napoleon returned to Germany with a new army of 200,000, all inexperienced conscripts, intending to separate the Allies and defeat them in detail. On 2 May he defeated an Allied army at Lützen, and captured Dresden. Sending Ney to outflank the retreating Allied army, Napoleon mounted a frontal assault. If Ney had attacked the Allied rear as was planned, French victory would have been complete, but he hesitated and the Allied commander, Wittgenstein, saved his army. Napoleon obtained a six weeks' armistice, in which time both sides prepared for the coming campaign. Napoleon was opposed by three armies, those of Blücher, who had replaced Wittgenstein, Schwarzenburg's Austrians (Austria having declared war on 12 August) and a Prusso-Swedish army under Bernadotte, ex-French marshal and now Crown Prince of Sweden; the latter army included a token British contingent.

On 26 August Schwarzenburg attacked the French at Dresden; Napoleon, though outnumbered, counter-attacked and won a brilliant tactical victory, but then fell into one of his strange spells of lethargy, and only one French corps, that of Vandamme, pursued the Allied army. Unsupported, Vandamme's corps was annihilated at Kulm (29–30 August). On 6 September, Ney's corps was defeated at Dennewitz when his Saxon contingent fled, and on 8 October Bavaria changed sides, leaving the Confederation of the Rhine for the Allies. On 16 October the Allies almost surrounded Napoleon at Leipzig in the 'Battle of the Nations'. For three days the French resisted frontal assaults, and when the Saxon corps deserted Napoleon was forced to retire. The bridge over the River Elster was blown prematurely, and Marshal Prince Poniatowski was drowned trying to swim across, another severe blow to the Grande Armée, which had lost 60,000 at Leipzig, as had the Allies. The one Allied setback was at Hanau, when a Bavarian army was defeated by Napoleon on 30 September–1 October. Foolishly rejecting an offer of peace, Napoleon forced the Allies to invade France. By November the Netherlands had revolted, and the Confederation of the Rhine had dissolved.

In Spain, 1813 was equally disastrous for the French. Wellington, now supreme commander of all Allied forces in the Iberian Peninsula, manoeuvred brilliantly, attacking King Joseph at Vittoria, the decisive battle of the war. The French army fled in confusion, after Wellington had pierced the centre and turned both flanks. Joseph, having lost his treasury and stores, fell back into France, as did Soult. An attempted counter-attack by Soult was repulsed at Sorauren, and the French were driven across the Pyrenees.

The Invasion of France

The Allies invaded France in 1814 in overwhelming numbers. In February, Napoleon threw back Blücher, defeating him four times in five days, in a manner reminiscent of the Napoleon of old; on 18 February he drove back Schwarzenburg at Montereau. At the end of February, Wellington defeated

Soult at Orthez, and captured Bordeaux on 17 March, the French retiring before him.

Napoleon continued his desperate attempt to postpone the inevitable defeat; despite his illness and the poor quality of his troops, his skill was that of old, which won the admiration even of his opponents. On 7 March Blücher was defeated at Craonne, but counter-attacked with overwhelming strength, forcing Napoleon back at Laon. Napoleon smashed a Prussian corps at Rheims (13 March) but Blücher and Schwarzenburg united in front of Paris. Marshals Marmont and Mortier resisted the Allied advance, but with only 22,000 men against 110,000, were forced back, and on 31 March Marmont surrendered Paris. At the suggestion of his marshals, Napoleon abdicated in favour of his son (6 April), but the Allies insisted upon his unconditional abdication (11 April). The last act of the war was played out on 10 April, when Wellington captured Toulouse.

Napoleon was granted the island of Elba, where he retired, the monarchy being restored in France. In 1815 Napoleon attempted to regain his throne, but was defeated by the combined armies of Wellington and Blücher in the 'Hundred Days' campaign, culminating with the Battle of Waterloo. Napoleon's exile to St. Helena ended the Napoleonic Wars, and with it ended the Emperor's dream of a unified state of Europe. But it was the beginning of the Napoleonic legend, a legend which grew throughout the nineteenth century, and which is even now still growing.

MILITARY UNIFORMS AND WEAPONS OF THE
NAPOLEONIC WARS

At the beginning of the French Revolutionary and Napoleonic Wars, the armies of Europe were costumed in a manner which had changed little since the wars of the eighteenth century. Basically, the armies of various states were uniformed in a similar pattern, only the colours distinguishing the nationality. The basic style consisted of a felt cocked hat, a long-skirted coat worn open to expose the waistcoat, breeches and gaiters or riding-boots in the case of cavalry. Varying 'arms of service' wore similar distinguishing features in all armies: the mitre-shaped fur cap of the Grena-diers, the more functional uniform of the light infantry, the fur caps and pelisses of the Hussars (a term originally used to describe Hungarian light cavalry), and the white uniform of the heavy cavalry of numerous German states. Armies were distinguished by basic uniform colours – white for France, Spain and Austria, red for Britain, blue for Prussia and green for Russia. Within individual armies, regiments were distinguished by different coloured 'facings', this term being applied to the collar, cuffs, lapels and sometimes the 'turnbacks' of the coat-tails.

The French Revolution began the transformation of military costume which continued to change the appearance of European armies with amazing rapidity until the late nineteenth century. The huge masses of conscripts required by the armies of Revolutionary France adopted the blue uniform of the National Guard, and the old white uniform of the French regulars was abandoned forever (except for an unsuccessful experi-ment in 1806–7). These changes in uniform began the rapid evolution which affected the armies of every participant in the wars of the next twenty years.

The first general changes became evident at the turn of the century. The old style of coat-tail became shorter, and in many cases the double-breasted coat gave way to a single-breasted version, closed to the waist. The cocked hat was replaced for all except officers in the majority of most armies by a 'shako', a cylindrical felt or leather headdress, usually with a peak, in a bewildering variety of styles, ornamented with metal badges, cockades, plumes and cords in abundance. The word 'shako' is derived from the Hungarian term for a peaked hat. By 1810 the shako was the most common headdress for the armies of Europe, though the traditional fur Grenadier cap was still prized by those élite corps privileged to wear it

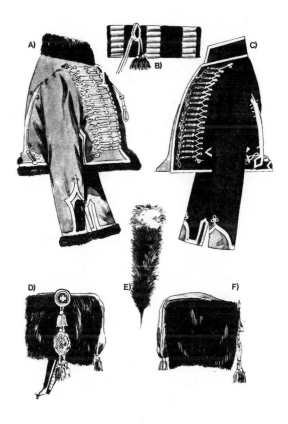

Figure 1. Chasseurs à Cheval of the Imperial Guard

A. Pelisse. Scarlet cloth with black fur trim. Orange lace and braiding for the rank and file, mixed green and gold lace and braiding for N.C.O.s. Officers had gold lace, and white fur trim.
B. 'Barrelled' sash. Green cloth, with cords, 'barrels' and tassels of distinctive colours : gold for officers, mixed scarlet and gold for N.C.O.s, and red for other ranks.
C. Dolman. Dark green with red cuffs. Gold lace for officers, mixed scarlet and gold for N.C.O.s, and orange for other ranks.
D. Colpack. See description of Figure E, Plate 4 (side view).
E. Plume. See description of Figure E, Plate 4.
F. Colpack. See description of Figure E, Plate 4 (front view).

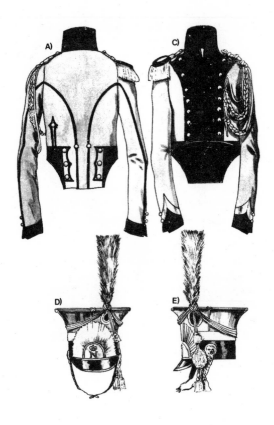

Figure 2. 2nd Chevau-Légers-Lanciers of the Imperial Guard ('The Red Lancers')

A & C. Trooper's Kurtka. Scarlet with dark blue facings and piping. Brass buttons. Yellow epaulette and aiguillette, the epaulette having a blue 'crescent'.

D & E. Trooper's czapka. Red cloth top, with black leather peak and turban. Yellow centre band and piping, yellow cords and tassels. Brass plate, peak-edging and brass chinscales on a red cloth backing. 'Tricolor' cockade and white plume. Officers wore a similar shako, but with gold lace, cords and piping; senior N.C.O.s had cords of mixed scarlet and gold.

(a variant is still worn by Britain's Brigade of Guards). Leather helmets with fur or woollen crests were favoured by several German states, notably Bavaria.

Cavalry uniforms were influenced by the large variety of corps raised in the French army: Hussars, Dragoons, Cuirassiers, Chasseurs à Cheval, Horse Grenadiers, Carabiniers and Lancers, each with a distinctive uniform and colouring, the Hussars as always retaining their resplendent colouring and in some cases their fur caps, which were also adopted by the Chasseurs à Cheval. The emergence of light infantry as an important force on the battlefield resulted in a new style of uniform, more functional and, of necessity, more sombre than before, to act as an early version of camouflage, though in the French army in particular this aspect was somewhat negated by the plumes and epaulettes in the yellow, red and green colours of the 'Voltigeur' arm.

The military fashion of Europe was to a large extent influenced by that of France. Those countries under French domination or alliance adopted costume of a totally French style, sometimes combining 'native' items with those of French origin. Even the opponents of France felt the influence of French fashions.

At the beginning of the period, the French uniform was in the cut of that of the 'Ancien Régime', with blue as the predominant colour. Although the legwear remained basically unchanged, the coat gradually became shorter, and in 1812 a jacket, closed to the waist, was adopted by the infantry, a direct influence of the Polish styles which had prevailed since the introduction of Polish troops in the late 1790s. The shako, which replaced the cocked hat in 1806–7, changed slightly over the years but retained its characteristic, slightly bell-topped form, which was extensively copied throughout Europe. Different types of infantry had varying distinctions – for example, the red plumes and epaulettes of the Grenadiers.

The neo-classical style of art popular in France resulted in the metal helmet worn by dragoons, cuirassiers, carabiniers and some of the Chevau-Légers-Lanciers, though the helmet had its origin in a peakless version worn before the Revolution. The cuirass, a return to the armour of the medieval period, had been adopted by several regiments of cavalry in Europe in the eighteenth century, but it was the formation of the cuirassier arm of the French army which brought about the general revival of armoured horsemen, the great 'shock weapon' of the Napoleonic Wars. The braided dolman and pelisse of the Hussar corps remained largely unchanged, but became progressively more splendid. Ironically, the most vital arm of service, the artillery, wore the plainest and least elaborate uniforms of the army; this was a custom prevalent throughout Europe.

Polish influence originated with the introduction of Polish exiles into the French service, and the square-topped 'czapka' headdress, the plastron-fronted 'kurtka' jacket, and the loose trousers soon became the accepted dress of cavalry regiments armed with the traditional Polish weapon, the lance, not only in France but throughout Europe, and Polish styles were gradually adopted by other arms.

British uniform developed independently until 1800, when the short-tailed infantry jacket and 'stove-pipe' shako were introduced. In 1812 the shako altered to the false-fronted 'Belgic' pattern, perhaps inspired by the earlier Portuguese 'Barretina' style. French influence was more keenly felt in the cavalry in 1812, when brass and leather helmets reminiscent of the French dragoon style were introduced into the heavy cavalry, while the light dragoons abandoned their uniquely British 'Tarleton' helmet and braided dolman for a bell-topped shako and Polish-style jacket. The Hussar costume became progressively more French in style, particularly when shakos were adopted. British influence was evident in Portugal, whose army was reorganised and to some extent officered by the British, and in Spain, whose uniforms had been the most outdated of any European state.

The Prussian army uniforms followed a natural progression from those of the famous days of Frederick the Great, but the collapse after Jena necessitated a complete reorganisation, and consequently a new style of uniform was evolved, consisting of a closed jacket and slightly bell-topped shako which became standard for the reconstructed Prussian army, though elements of the old uniform were retained.

Austrian uniforms, on the whole, changed little. The traditional white uniform was retained, together with a distinctively-shaped shako, though a leather-crested helmet was worn for a short time. Grenadiers retained their fur caps with large brass plates, and the Hungarian regiments their famous sky-blue breeches. In common with the other states, the Austrian hussars presented an impressive myriad of colours. Lancers were naturally costumed in the Polish style.

The early years of the nineteenth century were spent by Czar Alexander I in 'de-Prussianising' the Russian army, which involved a general re-organisation and a change in uniform which culminated in the distinctive scuttle-shaped 'kiwer' shako, probably designed by Alexander himself, though the traditional Russian green colour was retained. The Russian cuirassiers retained the white uniform common to much of the heavy cavalry of central Europe in the previous century, but added a tall leather helmet. A similar style was worn by the dragoons, whose basic colour was

Figure 3. French accoutrements

A.   Officer's sabretache, 10th Chasseurs à Cheval, Consulate period. Red cloth ground with gold lace and embroidery, and gold fringes.

B.   Officer's sabretache, service dress, Chasseurs à Cheval of the Imperial Guard. Black leather, bearing the Imperial arms in gilt metal.

C & D.   Epaulettes of the 'chef de bataillon' (Major), Grenadiers of the Imperial Guard. Gold lace and embroidery.

E.   Officer's full dress sabretache, sabre and belt, Chasseurs à Cheval of the Imperial Guard. Sabretache with green cloth ground with gold lace edging and fringe, bearing the Imperial Arms in natural colours (gold eagle and crown, on ermine backing with crimson lining and gold lace edging, medium blue flags with orange tips, on flagpoles which are coloured [reading from the centre out], medium blue, crimson and medium green). Red leather belt and slings with gold lace and gilt fittings. Sabre with gilt fittings and black leather scabbard, also fitted gilt. Gold sword-knot.

F.   Officer's pouch, Chasseurs à Cheval. Leather, with silvered flap bearing a hunting horn badge in gold, with gold lace edging.

G.   Pouch, Grenadiers of the Imperial Guard. Black leather, with brass badges. Fastened underneath is the fatigue cap ('bonnet de police'), which was dark blue with orange piping and tassel.

H.   Pouch, Grenadiers à Cheval of the Imperial Guard. Black leather with brass badge. Also worn by the Dragoons of the Imperial Guard.

Figure 4. French headdress

A. Undress cap ('bonnet de police'), officer, Chasseurs à Cheval of the Imperial Guard. Green cloth, with gold lace, tassel and badge, with red piping.

B. Officer's hat, Chasseurs à Cheval of the Imperial Guard. Black felt, with gold lace loop, gilt button, 'tricolor' cockade, and green plume with red tip.

C. Fusilier officer's shako, 81st Line Regiment, 1812 pattern. Black felt with leather reinforcements. Gilt plate and chinscales. 'Tricolor' cockade of white, red and blue (reading from the outside). White pompom with coloured surround and tuft: 1st company, green; 2nd company, sky blue; 3rd company, orange; 4th company, violet. Company number was borne in the centre of the cockade.

E. Colpack, Chasseurs à Cheval of the Imperial Guard. Black-brown fur with red 'bag'. Piping and tassel of bag and hanging cords or 'raquettes' of gold for officers, mixed green and gold for N.C.O.s, and orange for other ranks. Gilt chinscales for officers, brass for other ranks. 'Tricolor' cockade bearing small Imperial eagle badge. Green plume with a red tip for all except senior officers, who had white plumes.

F. Ornament worn on the rear of the bearskin caps of the Grenadiers of the Imperial Guard, 1808–15. Red cloth patch bearing gold grenade for officers and N.C.O.s, white grenade for other ranks. Prior to 1808, the red patch bore a white cross; from 1801–2 the cross was orange.

G. Shako plate, 81st Line Regiment, 1812 pattern. Gilt for officers, brass for other ranks.

24

green, and the Hussar costume relieved the otherwise sombre appearance of the Russian army.

The remaining combatants in the Napoleonic Wars based their designs on those of the larger powers. The states not under French influence adopted a combination of styles copied from those of Russia, Prussia and sometimes France, incorporating items of their own design, for example the Swedish 'kusket' helmet. Styles changed and interchanged, were copied and modified, until the result was a 'glittering panoply' of almost incredible dimensions.

Weapons and equipment, on the other hand, changed little throughout the period. The infantry private was equipped with leather 'cross-belts', supporting a black cartridge-pouch, a haversack, a bayonet, and in most continental armies, a short sword, which was a near-useless relic of the eighteenth century. On his back he carried a 'pack' or knapsack, which might be constructed of varnished leather, canvas or animal skin, in which he carried his spare clothing, food and few personal belongings. The total weight might be anything up to 60 pounds, which, coupled with his tight-fitting and unfunctional uniform, made simple movements difficult, let alone fighting. The cavalry had similar equipment, though much of theirs was carried on the saddle.

The basic weapon of the Napoleonic Wars was the smoothbore, flintlock musket, which generally had a maximum range of 250 yards, though it was wildly inaccurate at 100; approximately 250 musket balls were fired in battle for every man killed. The ball or bullet was a spherical piece of lead, which caused appalling wounds. Tactics were controlled by the weapons available, and the army of the Napoleonic period fought in compact blocks of troops, in which the individual was virtually transformed into an

---

H. Cors or 'raquettes' for colpack of Chasseurs à Cheval of the Imperial Guard.

I. Bearskin cap, Grenadiers of the Imperial Guard. Black bearskin, with a gilt plate for officers and copper for other ranks. The cords and tassels were gold for officers, mixed gold and scarlet for sergeants and senior N.C.O.s, and white for Grenadiers. Scarlet plumes worn by all ranks, except senior officers, who wore white. At the rear was borne the cloth patch shown in figure 'F'.

J. Cap plate, Grenadiers of the Imperial Guard, 1804–15. Gilt for officers, copper for other ranks.

automaton which loaded, aimed and fired until ordered to stop or until stopped by an enemy bullet. Disciplined troops could fire at a rate of two and a half to three shots per minute, though after a dozen shots the musket-barrel became progressively more fouled with burnt gunpowder, reducing the rate of fire to one shot or even less per minute. The bayonet, in effect a knife fixed on the end of the musket, was used for hand-to-hand combat; contrary to popular belief, a bayonet charge rarely took place on troops which were not already shattered by musketry, and the 'charge' was often conducted at a walk. The only defence against cavalry was to form a square, presenting a near-impregnable rectangle of bayonets to the enemy.

Light infantry was used for 'skirmishing', that is, extending in open order to harass the enemy, to precede an attack or absorb the first shock of the enemy advance. Certain corps were armed with rifled muskets, which were more accurate than the smoothbore; the success of this system is best shown by the British Light Division in the Peninsular War, undoubtedly a major factor in the French defeat.

The 'shock troops' of the Napoleonic army were the heavy cavalry, big men on big horses, frequently armoured, whose duty was to smash enemy formations and ride down broken regiments. Their swords were generally long and straight, made for thrusting. The lighter cavalry was used as a support for the heavy, and was also employed on reconnaissance and skirmishing. Cavalry charges were executed over short distances; only in the last fifty yards were the horses given their heads. Over difficult terrain, the 'charge' might be little more than a walk. Lances were particularly successful not only against cavalry, but a lancer could jab at a square with deadly effect, while keeping out of bayonet range. Cavalry firearms, carbines and pistols, were largely useless due to their short range.

The most powerful weapon on the field of battle was the artillery; cannon which fired 'roundshot' and howitzers which fired shells. The cast-iron cannon-ball was the principal weapon, travelling up to a mile, and capable of destroying a score of men. When bouncing and even rolling along the ground, a roundshot could carry away a limb. They came in numerous sizes, from the small four-pound ball to the giant twenty-eight-pounder. The cannon were named after the weight of ball they fired. Below 400 yards, cannon could be turned into huge shotguns by firing 'canister' or 'case-shot', a metal cylinder which ruptured at the muzzle of the gun, spreading its load of musket-balls over a wide arc. Howitzers fired spherical shells which exploded amid the enemy, fragmenting into shrapnel (only the British had shrapnel proper, their shells bursting over the heads of the enemy). Rockets were used by the British at Leipzig and Waterloo,

26

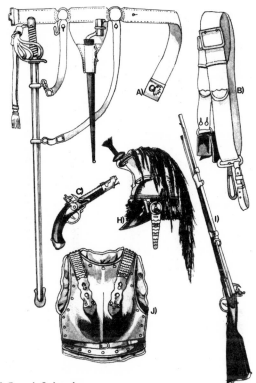

Figure 5. French Cuirassiers

A.   Sabre, bayonet and belt. White leather belt with brass plate and fittings.
     Sabre (model An XI) with brass hilt and steel scabbard. White sword-knot
     for the rank and file, mixed red and white for N.C.O.s, and gold lace for
     officers. Brown leather bayonet-scabbard, which was not carried by
     officers and senior N.C.O.s.
B.   Shoulder-belts. White leather with brass fittings, one supporting the black
     leather pouch, and one supporting the carbine. Carbine-belts not worn by
     officers or senior N.C.O.s.
C.   Pistol, model An IX. Steel barrel and lock, brass fittings.
H.   Helmet, 1811 pattern. Steel with crest, chinscales and plume socket of
     brass. Black fur band, black horsehair 'tail' and tuft (aigrette).
I.   Carbine, model An IX. Brass fittings. The loop for attachment to the carbine
     belt can be seen.
J.   Cuirass. Steel with brass rivets. Lined with red cloth with white edging.
     Tied at the waist by black leather belt. Brass scales with red cloth over the
     shoulders. Officers wore similar cuirasses, but with silver edging to the
     lining, red waist-belts edged silver, and gilt shoulder-scales.

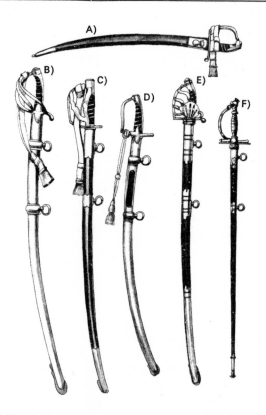

Figure 6. French Swords

A. Sabre, Grenadiers of the Consular Guard. Short sword carried by the rank
    and file only. Brass hilt, black leather scabbard with brass fittings. White
    sword-knot with red tassel for all except senior N.C.O.s, who had knots of
    mixed scarlet and gold. Black leather grip bound with wire.
B. Light cavalry sabre, *c*. 1812. Brass hilt, steel scabbard. Black leather grip
    bound with wire.
C. Chasseur à Cheval sabre, *c*. 1801. Brass hilt, black leather scabbard with
    brass fittings. Black leather hilt bound with wire.
D. Chasseur à Cheval of the Imperial Guard, *c*. 1812. Brass hilt, black leather
    grip bound with wire. Brass scabbard with black leather inserts. Gold
    sword-knot for officers, white leather for other ranks.
E. Officer's sabre, Dragoons, *c*. 1812. Brass hilt, black leather grip bound
    with wire. Black leather scabbard with brass fittings.
F. General Officer's sword, *c*. 1812. Gilt hilt. Black leather scabbard with gilt
    fittings.

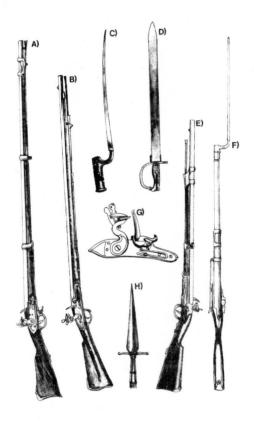

Figure 7. Weapons

A. French musket, Infantry of the Imperial Guard. Brass fittings.
B. British Infantry musket, nicknamed 'Brown Bess'. Brass fittings.
C. British socket bayonet for the 'Brown Bess' musket. Steel, carried in a black leather scabbard.
D. British sword-bayonet for the Baker Rifle, 2nd pattern, 1801–*c.* 1815. Brass hilt; carried in a black leather scabbard with brass fittings.
E. French Hussar carbine. Brass fittings.
F. French carbine, Chasseurs à Cheval of the Imperial Guard, with fixed bayonet.
G. The flintlock mechanism.
H. British 'spontoon' head; a 'half-pike' carried by sergeants of infantry.

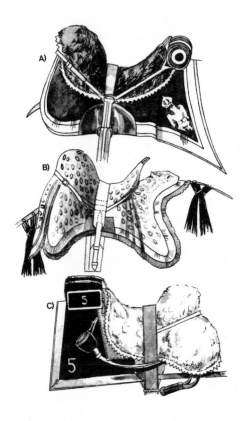

Figure 8. French shabraques

A. 2nd Chevau-Légers-Lanciers of the Imperial Guard. Dark blue cloth with yellow lace and ornaments. Scarlet valise with yellow lace and piping. Black sheepskin saddle-cover edged with yellow. Black leather straps. Officers had similar shabraques, but with gold lace, a pantherskin saddle cover, and red leather straps.

B. Chasseurs à Cheval of the Imperial Guard. Officer's shabraque of pantherskin, edged with a band on gold lace with red piping on either side of the lace, and a green cloth outer edge.

C. 5th Cuirassiers. Blue shabraque and valise with white piping and numerals. White sheepskin saddle-cover trimmed with the regimental facing colour (light orange). Black leather straps.

but were unreliable and only effective in weakening the morale of the enemy.

Compared to arms of the present age, the weapons of the Napoleonic period were in their infancy. But sabre, musket-ball and roundshot could inflict hideous wounds, and kill, maim and slaughter with appalling efficiency; in the Italian campaign of 1943–44, from the landings at Salerno to the fall of Rome, the Allied Fifth Army lost scarcely any more men than the French lost at Borodino in eleven hours, on a front of three and a half miles.

INTRODUCTION TO THE COLOUR PLATES

The study of military costume is a most inexact science. There are three basic sources from which information on military uniforms may be obtained: firstly, actual items of uniform and equipment still in existence; these are, at this distance in time, very scarce. Secondly, there are 'dress regulations'; and thirdly, pictures by contemporary artists. These three sources, however, more often than not present conflicting evidence. Dress regulations, where they existed at all, were frequently and flagrantly disregarded; officers often incorporated features of their own design into regulation uniform, and it was not uncommon for whole regiments to wear items of uniform not officially recognised. This applies equally to pieces of uniform still in existence; a coat, for example, may include a feature unique to the officer to whom it belonged. To complicate matters further, some contemporary artists were less accurate than others, and the uniforms they sketched might contain features adopted on campaign.

When on campaign, uniforms quickly changed their appearance when non-regulation items of uniform were adopted of necessity. To give an example of how a regiment's uniforms might incorporate unusual features, take the extreme case of the British 95th Rifles in Spain in 1812; Lieutenant George Simmons described them as 'a moving rag-fair'. John Kincaid, another officer of the 95th, described his regiment: 'there was scarcely a vestige of uniform among the men, some of whom were dressed in Frenchmen's coats, some in white breeches and huge jack-boots, some with cocked hats and queues; most of their swords were fixed on the rifles, and stuck full of hams, tongues, and loaves of bread, and not a few were carrying bird-cages! There never was a better masked corps!' Rifleman Edward Costello also described them 'dressed in all the varieties imaginable, some with jack-boots on, others with frock-coats, epaulettes, &c., and some even with monkeys on their shoulders. . . . I was afterwards told by several of our men that the Duke of Wellington, who saw us on our march, inquired of his staff, "who the devil are those fellows?" .' Costello himself wore a pair of trousers captured from a French dragoon, while Kincaid had two pairs of trousers, one made of common brown Portuguese cloth, and one of black velvet which he wore on Sundays!

For these reasons, it is extremely difficult to say with absolute accuracy exactly what was worn by a regiment at a particular time, beyond the general pattern of uniform. Some of the uniforms illustrated in the following plates may not agree with other recognised authorities, but all have been checked against their sources.

1 France: 4th Hussars. Troopers, 1796 and 1790

2 Russia: Chevaliers Garde. Officer *(left)* and N.C.O. *(right)*, 1796

3 Switzerland: Light Cavalry. Trooper *(left)* and Officer *(right)*, *c.* 1800

4 Poland: Artillery. Gunners, 1799 and 1808

5 Saxony: Kurfürst Cuirassier Regiment. Trooper *(left)* and Officer *(right)*, 1803

6 Britain: The King's German Legion. Hussar Officer *(left)* and Infantry
Private *(right), c.* 1813

7 France: Hussars. Troopers, *c.* 1807

8/9 **France: Marshals.** *(Left to right)* Undress Foot, Undress M

ted, Full dress Foot, with greatcoat, Marshall Bessières, c. 1805

10 Switzerland: Volunteer Jägers of Zurich. Riflemen, *c.* 1805

11 France: Cuirassiers. Troopers, 1812

12 **Baden: Hussars.** Officers, 1812

13 **Nassau: Jägers.** Officers, *c.* 1807

14 France: 33rd Regiment of Infantry. Privates *(left and centre)* and
N.C.O. *(right)*, 1807

15 Holland: Private. 3rd Light Infantry *(left)* and Officer 2nd Line Infantry *(right)*, *c.* 1807

16 France: Mameluke. Trooper, 1806

17 Spain: Villaviciosa Dragoons. Trooper, *c.* 1806

18 Saxony: Guard Grenadiers. Privates, *c.* 1806

19 France: Dragoons. Officer 17th Regiment *(left)* and Officer 4th Regiment *(right)*, *c.* 1812

20 **Sweden: Royal Life Guards.** Trooper *(left)* and Officer *(right)*, 1807

21 Denmark: King's Life Rifle Corps. Riflemen *(left and centre)* and
Officer *(right)*, 1807

22 Sweden: Life Grenadier Regiment and Grenadier Corps.
Officers, c. 1813

23 Italy: Guard of Honour. Troopers, Bologna *(left)*, Rome *(centre)* and Milan *(right)*, c. 1808

24/25 **Italy: Guard of Honour.** *(Left to right)* Officer in full dress, mo
Officers in full

ed, Officer in stable dress, Trooper in stable dress, Officer in undress cape coat,
ss, unmounted, c. 1808

26 Spain: Guerrillas, *c.* 1809

27 France: Chasseurs à Cheval of the Guard. Trooper, 1808

28 Württemburg: Garde Jäger Squadron. Officer, *c.* 1808

29 **Prussia: 2nd Life Hussars.** Trooper *(left)* and Officer *(right), c.* 1809

30 Portugal: Caçadores. Corporal 4th Battalion *(left)* and Private 5th
Battalion *(right)*, 1808

31 Prussia: General Staff. Parade dress *(left)*, King's Adjutant-General *(centre)* and Cavalry Service dress *(right)*, 1808-12

32 **Austria: Hungarian Grenadiers.** Officer *(left)*, Private *(centre)* and Officer *(right)* 1814

33 Saxe-Coburg-Saalfeld Infantry. Service dress *(left)* and Review
Order *(right)*, 1809

34 Russia: Jäger Regiments. Officers, 1809

35 **France: Portuguese Legion.** Cavalry Officer *(left)* and Infantry
Officer *(right)*, *c.* 1809

36 France: Geographical Engineers. Officers, *c.* 1809

37 **Bavaria**: Sharpshooter *(left)* **Preysing Regiment.** and Grenadier *(right)*, **Leib Regiment.** 1809

38 Prussia: Garde Jäger Battalion. Jager *(left)* and Officer *(right)*, 1809

39 Austria: Grenadiers. Officer *(left)* and Private *(right)*, 1809

40/41 **Britain:** *(Left to right)* Officer, Priv

mounted General Officer and Officer, 1809

42 **The Brunswick Corps.** Jager *(left)* and
Infantry Private *(right)*, 1809

43 France: Chasseurs à Cheval of the Line. Troopers, Elite Company
1st Regiment, 1810

44 Westphalia: Garde du Corps. Officer, 1810

45 Switzerland: Légion Sainte-Galloise. Privates, 1810

46 **Bavaria and Saxony: Surgeons.** Bavarian *(left)* and Saxon *(right)*,
1810

47 France: Engineers of the Imperial Guard. Privates *(left and centre)* and Officer *(right)*, 1810

48 France: Infantry of the Vistula Legion, c. 1810

49 Hesse-Darmstadt: Chevau-Légers, Trooper,1810

50 **France: 2nd Chevau-Légers-Lanciers of the Imperial Guard.**
Trooper *(left)*, Officer in Campaign dress *(centre)* and Trooper *(right)*, 1810

51 Britain: 2nd Greek Light Infantry. Privates, 1813

52 **Saxony: Jägercorps** 1813 **and Light Infantry** 1810

53 **France: 1st (Polish) Chevau-Légers-Lanciers of the Imperial Guard.** Trooper mounted *(left)* and Officer *(right)*, 1811

54 Spain: 7th Regiment Lancers of La Mancha. Trooper, *c.* 1811

55 France: Valaison Battalion. *c.* 1810

56/57 **France: Neuchâtel Battalion.** *(Left to right)* (

er, Gunner, Driver, Engineer Private and Officer, *c*. 1812

58 France: 30th Chasseurs à Cheval. Officers, 1811

59 Poland: General Officers. Parade dress *(left)* and Undress *(right),*
c. 1796

60 **Saxony: Chevau-Légers.** Polentz Regiment Officer *(left)* and Prince
Clement Regiment Officer *(right)*, 1812

61 Britain: 10th Royal Hussars. Trooper, 1812

62 **France: Corsican Regiment** . Officer *(left)*, Carabinier
(centre) and Voltigeur *(right)*, *c.* 1812

63 France: Lithuanian Tartars. Trooper, c. 1812

64 France: Grenadiers of the Imperial Guard. *c.* 1812

65 Duchy of Warsaw: The Krakus. Officers, *c*. 1812

66 **France: The Isembourg Regiment.** Carabiniers *(left and centre)* and
Voltigeur Officer *(right).* c. 1811

67 Cleve-Berg: Infantry. Officer *(left)* and Grenadiers *(centre and right)*,
c. 1812

68 **Bavaria: Foot Artillery,** Officer *(left)* and Private *(right)*, *c.* 1812

69 **Prussia: 10th (Colberg) Regiment.** Grenadier *(left)* and Musketeer *(right)*, 1812

70 Britain: 42nd Royal Highland Regiment. Officer *(left)* and Private *(right)*, *c.* 1812

71 France: Aides de Camp. Officers, *c.* 1812

72/73 **Russia: Cuirassiers.** *(Left to right)* N.C.O Czarina's Regimen
Trooper Pskoff Regiment, O

ounted Officer Pskoff Regiment, Officer Military Order Regiment, mounted
r Klein Russland Regiment, 1812

74 Russia: Infantry. Musketeer *(left)* and Grenadier *(right)*, 1812

75 Württemburg: Artillery. Officer *(left)*, Private *(centre)* and Officer, *c.* 1812

76 **France: 4th Swiss Infantry.** Officers, 1812

77 Saxony: Garde du Corps. Officer, *c.* 1812

78 Hanover: Feldjägercorps von Kielmannsegge. Sharpshooter *(left)* and Rifleman *(right) c.* 1814

79 Prussia: Landwehr Infantry. *c.* 1814

80 **Russia: Light Infantry.** Carabinier *(left)* Jäger Private *(centre)* and
Carabinier *(right)*, *c.* 1814

1. France: 4th Hussars.
Troopers, 1796 and 1790

The corps of Hussars raised in 1783 as the 'Colonel-Général' Regiment became the 4th Hussars of the French Republic following the Revolution. The uniform changed very little from then until 1815, except that the style followed the trends of military fashion.

The uniform was typical of the hussar style: the braided dolman or jacket; the fur-lined pelisse, which could be worn either hanging from the shoulder, as illustrated, or as a coat; the tight breeches and 'Hessian' boots (frequently replaced on active service by overalls), the 'barrelled' sash (crimson with yellow 'barrels' or bars of braid for the 4th), and the sabretache suspended from the sword-belt. The headdress shown in this plate, the 'mirliton' cap, was a cylindrical, peakless shako, which had a long tail or streamer of coloured cloth worn round the body of the cap and allowed to hang loose down the wearer's back.

Two uniforms are shown; the right-hand figure is in the uniform of 1790, when the regiment was still wearing the dress of the latter days of the Ancien Régime; the sabretache bears the cipher of King Louis XVI. This design was changed under the Republican government to one of the lictor's fasces within a wreath of laurel. The left-hand figure shows the uniform of 1796; by this time the plume on the mirliton had become red over black. Both figures are troopers; officers wore basically the same uniform, but with gold lace instead of yellow.

After distinguished service in the Napoleonic Wars, the regiment was amalgamated with the 13th and 14th Hussars to form the new 4th Hussars, the 'Hussards de Monsieur'.

2. Russia: Chevaliers Garde.
Officer and N.C.O., 1796

Raised by Peter the Great as a sixty-man royal bodyguard, the Chevaliers Garde was the most distinguished unit in the Russian service. It served as a palace guard until 1800, when its strength was increased from a squadron to a regiment, and became the senior corps of cuirassiers in the Russian army. The uniforms depicted are conspicuously Prussian in pattern.

The bicorn hat was made of black felt, with silver tassels at the corners; the plumes were white over orange for officers, and orange over white for other ranks. The hat bore the black and orange cockade of Imperial Russia. The coatee, of the traditional white, had a 'stand-and-fall' collar in the red facing colour, and was edged with silver lace. The breast of the coatee was ornamented by a band of silver lace, with a red edging on either side.

The officer is shown wearing a 'supreveste', a sleeveless coat cut to resemble a cuirass. This was of black cloth for other ranks, of velvet for officers, and was edged red, with silver piping for officers. After 1800, when Czar Paul I became Grand Master of the Order of St. John of Jerusalem, the 'supreveste' was embellished with a large white Maltese Cross on the front.

The white breeches and high black boots were those worn for full dress; grey overalls were frequently adopted on service. The swords at this time had guards in the form of an eagle; the sword-hilt later changed to one of gilt for officers and copper for other ranks. The sabretache and shabraque, or saddle-cloth, were red edged with silver lace, and bearing the Star of the Order of St. Andrew. The officers' pouches were of black leather, bearing a plate of silver in the form of the Star of the Order of St. Andrew, the pouch-belt being silver lace edged orange.

In 1802 a double-breasted white jacket was introduced, and in 1803 a tall black leather helmet with a brass plate (gilt for officers) and a woollen 'caterpillar' crest. In 1808 this crest was replaced by one of horsehair, though officers wore the old woollen pattern until 1811. Epaulettes were introduced in 1807. In 1812, as befitted the senior regiment of cuirassiers, black enamelled cuirass-fronts (worn without a backplate) were issued to all ranks. On certain social occasions officers wore a red coatee with black facings, and there existed also a green uniform worn on occasion on active service.

3. Switzerland: Light Cavalry. Trooper and Officer, c. 1800

The Swiss Republic, proclaimed in 1798, based its uniforms on the red, gold and green 'national' colours. The cavalry of the new state were formed as 'chevaulégers' or light cavalry, their uniforms being cut in hussar style, and modelled on the French prototype.

The mirliton cap of the trooper shows the plume and streamer in the national colours. The green dolman was faced with red, and trimmed with yellow lace. On each side of the breast was a panel of eight bars of yellow lace, joined at the end of each bar by a vertical strip of lace. The dolman was worn open to show a red waistcoat, laced in a similar manner as the dolman. The waist sash was also red. The green tight-fitting breeches were decorated on the thighs by yellow lace in the form of 'Austrian knots'. The sword carried was a typical 'light cavalry' pattern, with a stirrup-hilt and a slightly curved blade. The horse furniture consisted of a shabraque of white sheepskin, edged with red cloth in a 'wolf's tooth' pattern.

The officer is shown in basically the same uniform, but with all the lace and braiding in gold instead of yellow. The headdress illustrated is a peakless felt shako, bound in black leather, and ornamented by green cords. The plume was in the national colours. The dolman worn was a more conventional pattern than that of the trooper, with fifteen rows of gold cord on the breast, each row having five gilt buttons. The pockets on each side were also decorated with gold cord. The 'Austrian knots' on the cuffs and thighs were of a more elaborate form than those worn by the other ranks. The officer illustrated does not wear the more usual 'Hessian' boots, but black cloth gaiters, buttoned up the side, worn over black shoes. The sabretache, supported by brown leather straps with gilt fittings, bears the cipher 'RH', representing 'Republique Helvétique', in gold embroidery on the green cloth face of the sabretache.

4. Poland: Gunner, Polish Danube Legion, 1799; and Officer, Horse Artillery of the Grand Duchy of Warsaw, 1808

Following the Third Partition of Poland in 1796, Polish emigrants entered the service of the newly-created Italian states under French domination. The left-hand figure represents a Gunner of the Artillery detachment of the Polish Danube Legion, which fought with the French in Italy from 1798 until 1800. The uniform worn was a mixture of French and Polish styles, the original headdress being the typically Polish 'czapka'. However, in the latter days of the existence of the Legion, the French-style shako as illustrated was adopted. The remainder of the uniform was cut on the lines of that of the French Hussars, and resembled the

uniform of the French Horse Artillery. The dolman worn was longer than usual, and worn open to show the waistcoat underneath, which had a collar and was braided in the same manner as the dolman.

In 1807, following the Treaties of Tilsit, the Grand Duchy of Warsaw was created as one of Napoleon's satellite states, with an army formed on French lines. The Horse Artillery of the Duchy was raised by Count Potocki in 1808, with the strength of one company, clothed and equipped at the Count's own expense. A second company was added in 1809, and in 1810, by a Royal Decree of the King of Saxony, the corps was increased to regimental strength of 690 men. The regiment served valiantly in the Russian campaign of 1812, suffered heavily, and became disorganised. By 1813 the strength had dwindled to three batteries, and when in 1814 the corps was reorganised, only one battery could be mustered.

The right-hand figure shows an officer of the Horse Artillery of the Duchy in 1808. The headdress is the uniquely Polish 'czapka', a type of shako with curved sides and a square top, a pattern which was copied by many European states in the nineteenth century as the headdress for regiments of lancers. The jacket also was typically Polish, with curved lapels and pointed cuffs. This uniform was worn until 1810, when the traditional Polish style was abandoned, and the corps was clothed in the same pattern as the

French Chasseurs à Cheval, complete with fur busbies.

5. Saxony: Kurfürst Cuirassier Regiment. Trooper and Officer (undress), 1803

In 1803 the Elector of Saxony, Frederick Augustus III, allied with Prussia against the French. The heavy cavalry of Saxony consisted at this time of three regiments, one of Carabiniers, and the Cuirassier Regiments of Kurfürst and Kochtitzky. The uniforms of these corps were largely eighteenth century in style, conforming to those worn by the armies of Prussia and Austria, i.e. a white coat, bicorn hat, black enamelled cuirass with brass rivets (of which only the front plate was worn), and high black boots.

Plate 5 shows the uniform of the Kurfürst Cuirassier Regiment in 1803. The trooper's dress is typical of the late eighteenth-century style favoured by central European armies. On the shabraque corners and the holster-caps can be seen the crowned 'F A' monogram of Frederick Augustus, though some contemporary pictures show the shabraque without this ornamentation.

The officer is shown wearing the sky-blue coat worn in undress uniform; in parade dress, officers wore a coat similar in cut to those of the other ranks, but in pale yellow, with red facings and gold lace. The officers' sashes were silver, with crimson horizontal stripes and large tassels; their

shabraques were red, edged with gold lace.

After the defeat of Prussia in 1806, Saxony allied with Napoleon, Frederick Augustus III becoming nominal ruler of Poland in 1807 as Duke of Warsaw. Saxony remained loyal to Napoleon even after the defeat at Leipzig in 1813. In 1810 the old-style uniforms were abandoned when the Saxon heavy cavalry was reorganised into three new regiments, the Gardes du Corps, the Garde Cuirassiers, and the Zastrow Cuirassiers. These new corps were clothed in French-inspired uniforms, though the traditional white colour was retained.

6. Britain: The King's German Legion. Officer, 1st Hussars, and Grenadier, line infantry, c. 1813

In the wars of 1801–6, the state of Hanover, closely connected to the British Crown, was alternately occupied by both France and Prussia. In August 1803, King George III charged Baron Friedrich von der Decken with the raising of a corps of infantry, to be formed in the Isle of Wight from Hanoverian citizens, and called the King's German Regiment.

Recruiting, however, was so good that by December the corps had been enlarged to an establishment of eight battalions of infantry, two of light infantry, two regiments of dragoons, three of light dragoons, and batteries of horse and foot artillery. In 1813 the cavalry was reorganised, the two dragoon regiments becoming light dragoons, and the three light dragoon regiments becoming hussars.

Recruiting was not limited to Hanoverians, Europeans of all nationalities (except French and Italians) being accepted. From 1806 to 1815 the Legion was in action continuously, in the Peninsular War and in Europe, performing magnificently throughout. No corps ever had a service record like that of the Legion, its career highlighted by such epics as the charge at Garcia Hernandez (1812) and the defence of La Haye Sainte at Waterloo.

The officer in Plate 6 wears a British-style hussar uniform, with the exception of the headdress, a unique peaked busby worn only by the Legion, the Hussar regiments of which also wore more conventional busbies and 'bell-topped' shakos. The Grenadier shows the uniform of the infantry battalions of the Legion after the introduction of the 'Belgic' shako in 1812, with the grey overalls as worn on campaign. All the line infantry battalions of the Legion wore the blue facings of a British 'royal' regiment, the uniforms being identical in cut to those of the British infantry. Equipment was of the standard pattern of the British army, though some sources show the Legion with packs of dark blue instead of the usual black. The Grenadier companies (of which there was one per battalion) were distinguished by white plumes and the shoulder 'wings' of white worsted.

Ordinary 'centre' companies of infantry battalions wore small worsted tufts instead of the large wings, and white over red plumes. The light companies of infantry (one per battalion) had similar wings to the Grenadiers, but with green plumes and shako-cords. The two light battalions wore green uniforms, similar to those of the British rifle regiments. The costume of the dragoons and light dragoons also conformed to the regulations of their counterparts in the British army.

7. France: Hussars. Trooper, Elite Company, 2nd Regiment, and Trooper, 9th Regiment, c. 1807

The Hussars were the most colourful branch of the French army, a full volume being needed to do justice to the history of their uniforms. Briefly, the cut of the uniform changed little from that shown in Plate 1, excepting the headdress; shakos were adopted in the early 1800s, the 1805 pattern having a large tricolor cockade on the front instead of a plate. The diamond-shaped plate illustrated was adopted in 1807; the 1810 Regulations again changed the design of plate to one in the form of an Imperial eagle. In 1813–14 the pattern of shako itself was changed to a taller, cylindrical version.

The uniform of each regiment differed in many ways; the chart below gives some very basic details of the uniform of the Hussar regiment from 1800 to 1812:

Regt.	Dolman	Collar	Cuffs	Pelisse	Breeches	Lace	Plumes
1	sky blue	sky blue	red	sky blue	sky blue	white	black
2	brown	brown	sky blue	brown	sky blue	white	black
3	grey	grey	red	grey	grey	red	black
4	blue	blue	red	red	blue	yellow	black
5	sky blue	sky blue	white	white	sky blue	yellow	white
6	red	red	red	blue	blue	yellow	black with red tip
7	green	red	red	green	red	yellow	black
8	green	red	red	green	red	white	black
9	red	sky blue	sky blue	sky blue	sky blue	yellow	black, white tip
10	sky blue	red	red	sky blue	sky blue	white	black, red base
11	blue	red	red	blue	blue	yellow	black
12	red	sky blue	sky blue	sky blue	sky blue	white	black, yellow tip
13	brown	brown	sky blue	brown	sky blue	white	black

The shakos were black (sky blue for the 5th and red for the 6th) with cords and tassels in the colour of the lace. The pelisses were trimmed with black fur for all regiments except the 11th, which wore white. All the pelisses were lined with white except those of the 11th, which were lined with red. The barrel sashes were crimson with barrels in the colour of the lace, with the following exceptions: the 3rd wore crimson sashes with white barrels, the 8th crimson with green, and the 11th crimson with white barrels, with a vertical blue line down the centre of the white.

The Elite companies wore fur busbies or colpacks, with or without red cords, and with red plumes. The 'bags' of the colpacks were red for the 1st, 4th, 6th, 7th, 8th and 10th, sky blue for the 2nd, 5th and 9th, and white for the 3rd.

Officers wore the same uniform colours as the other ranks, but gold or silver lace in place of the yellow or white (silver lace for officers of the 3rd). They wore crimson pouch and waist belts edged with lace, in place of the white of the other ranks. The design of sabretache varied greatly between regiments, though the design illustrated, an Imperial eagle within a laurel wreath with the regimental number, was the most common.

8/9. France: Marshals. Undress (dismounted), Undress (mounted), Full dress, with greatcoat, Marshal Bessières

The rank of Marshal of France was abolished in 1793, but on the creation of the French Empire in 1804, Napoleon reinstated the rank, promoting eighteen distinguished French officers to the rank of Marshal. The original creation of 9 May 1804 was: Augerau, Bernadotte, Berthier, Bessières, Brune, Davout, Jourdan, Kellermann, Lannes,

Lefebvre, Masséna, Moncey, Mortier, Murat, Ney, Perignon, Serurier and Soult. Other officers were promoted to Marshal later; Victor in 1807, Macdonald, Marmont and Oudinot in 1809, Suchet in 1811, St. Cyr in 1813 and Grouchy in 1815. This list embraces twenty-five of the most famous commanders of the age.

The uniform of Marshal of France had a simple grandeur; the coatee was dark blue throughout, heavily embroidered with gold wire in a design of oak leaves. This design was repeated on the gilt buttons, which also bore the symbol of the rank of Marshal, crossed batons. On State occasions, the coatee was replaced by a coat with longer tails, embroidered in the same manner. Gold wire epaulettes were worn on both. When on foot, the white breeches were worn with silk stockings and buckle shoes; when mounted, with riding-boots. Gold sashes were worn in all orders of dress; where the bullion tassels joined the sash it was usual to have an embroidered design of crossed batons, stars or an eagle. Bicorn hats were worn, with or without gold lace edging, and decorated along the inside edge with ostrich feathers. Shabraques were crimson with gold lace. The type of sword carried was a matter of personal choice, though the regulation pattern (as shown on the mounted figure) was richly decorated with gold embossing. The scarlet sashes and breast stars are those of the Order of the Legion of Honour.

Some Marshals, however, wore uniforms of their own design, often combining the uniform of their particular corps with the embellishments of Marshal's rank. Marshal Bessières is shown wearing the uniform of the Chasseurs à Cheval of the Imperial Guard, in his position as Commander of the Guard cavalry. He is shown holding the symbol of his rank, the Marshal's baton, which was covered in blue velvet, embroidered with thirty-two gold eagles. The ends of the baton were in engraved gilt brass; the top bore the Latin motto, 'Terror Belli Decus Pacis', the bottom the name of the Marshal and the date of his creation.

10. Switzerland: Zürich Volunteer Jäger Corps, c. 1805

The term 'Jäger' is German, originally being used to describe light infantry and 'rifle' troops who acted as skirmishers and scouts. The function of 'Jäger' corps was to fight in 'open order', harassing the enemy formations before an attack, or covering a retreat. The earliest forms of camouflage were adopted of necessity by these corps, green being the commonest colour, in order to make the Jägers as inconspicuous as possible. The system was copied with great success by the French, who employed their 'Voltigeurs' in the same manner, and by the British, whose 95th Rifle Regiment was perhaps the finest corps of all.

The figures illustrated show the

typical Jäger uniform, green with black facings, and devoid of all unnecessary adornments. The green plume was a universally-used symbol for light infantry. The entire uniform was as functional as contemporary military fashion would allow, even the epaulettes being reduced to simple shoulder-straps to keep the cross-belts in position.

The belts were white for all ranks except the sharpshooters, whose equipment was all black, to further assist camouflage. The sharpshooters were also distinguished by red Austrian knots on the thighs. Both the figures illustrated carried brass-hilted swords in addition to their muskets and bayonets.

The armband or 'brassard' worn by the right-hand figure is a feature of many Swiss uniforms of this period, being also worn by several of the Swiss regiments which entered British service.

11. France: Cuirassiers. Troopers, 10th, 4th and 5th Regiments, 1812

Prior to 1801, the French army contained only one regiment of cuirassiers, the 8th Cavalry. In 1802, the 2nd to 7th Regiments of Cavalry were also issued with steel cuirasses and helmets, and on 24 September 1803 all twelve regiments of heavy cavalry were officially converted to cuirassiers (though some were not equipped as such until the following year). In 1809 the 13th and 14th Regiments were formed, the latter from the 2nd Dutch Cuirassiers. In the years that followed, the cuirassiers were to become known as the finest heavy cavalry in Europe. The illustration shows the uniform adopted in 1809; prior to that date the coat-tails were longer. The coats were distinguished by facing colours arranged in the following order (1812):

Regiment	Collar and Turnbacks	Cuffs	Cuff-flaps
1	Red	Red	Red
2	Red	Red	Blue
3	Red	Blue	Red
4	Orange	Orange	Orange
5	Orange	Orange	Blue
6	Orange	Blue	Orange
7	Yellow	Yellow	Yellow
8	Yellow	Yellow	Blue
9	Yellow	Blue	Yellow
10	Pink	Pink	Pink
11	Pink	Pink	Blue
12	Pink	Blue	Pink
13	Carmine	Carmine	Carmine
14	Carmine	Carmine	Blue

The steel helmets, with crest and chin-scales of brass, were ringed with black fur, and ornamented with black horse-hair. In full dress, red plumes were worn by all ranks except senior officers, who wore white. White or cream breeches were worn in full dress, as shown on the right-hand figure; on campaign grey or brown overalls were adopted, as worn by the central figure. The red epaulettes and grenade badges on the turnbacks were the symbols of a 'corps d'élite'. In 1811 carbines and cartridge boxes were issued; the carbine was carried on the saddle, or worn hooked on a shoulder-belt, which can be seen on the central figure. Shabraques were dark blue for all regiments, distinguished only by the regimental number on the rear corners and on the portmanteau.

12. Baden: Hussars. Officers, 1812

The state of Baden allied with France in 1806, as part of the Confederation of the Rhine. The uniforms of its army were thereafter modelled on French lines.

The Baden Hussar regiment was ·a magnificent corps, probably one of the finest in Europe. Serving in the Russian campaign of 1812, the regiment was ordered, on 28 November, to protect the rear of the French army as the river Beresina was crossed. Together with the Hessian Chevau-Légers, the Baden Hussars attacked an overwhelming body of Russians at Studianka in the famous 'Charge of Death', from which only fifty men from each regiment survived. The sacrifice of the Baden Hussars, however, saved the Grande Armée.

The uniform was copied from that of the French hussars, with shako, dolman, pelisse, tight breeches, and even to the green Hessian boots worn by officers in full dress. The dismounted figure shows how the pelisse could be worn as a coat as an alternative to being slung over the left shoulder. The sabretache and rear corners of the shabraque bore the monogram of the Grand Duke of Baden, 'C F'.

On active service, the shako-plumes were discarded, grey overalls were worn in place of the breeches, and knee-length green coats, devoid of lace, replaced the dolman and pelisse.

13. Nassau: Jägers. Officers, c. 1807

In 1806 the states of Nassau–Weilburg and Nassau–Usingen allied with France by joining the Confederation of the Rhine. The total strength of the army of these small states comprised two regiments of infantry and one of mounted Jägers.

The mounted Jäger corps was raised, with a strength of one troop, in Nassau–Weilburg in 1804, being composed entirely of volunteers. In 1807 the strength was increased to two troops of 125 men each. The corps was nicknamed 'The Green Riders'.

Dark green uniforms were introduced for the army of Nassau in 1803, and were worn by the Jägers. The silver-laced dolman and breeches were influenced by the style of the French Hussars, but the headdress was the 'raupenhelm' pattern introduced into the Bavarian army in 1803. The helmet had a body of black leather, bound with white metal, and topped by a large 'raupe' or crest of black bearskin. The helmet plate on the front bore the arms of Nassau, and the green plume symbolised the function of the corps.

As befitted a corps of Jägers, the rank and file were armed with carbines, and the equipment was of black leather. Black leather sabretaches were sometimes worn; these carried a silver badge of the crowned 'F.A.' (Friedrich Augustus) monogram, which was also borne on the pouch. The sombre appearance of the corps was further enforced by the shabraques of black lambskin and the black leather harness.

The Regiment had by 1810 adopted a uniform of the French Chasseurs à Cheval style, complete with fur colpacks or busbies.

14. France: 33rd Regiment of Infantry. Grenadiers and Quartermaster, 1807

Prior to the Revolution, white had been the traditional colour of the French regular army, but in the 1790s the blue of the National Guard was adopted by all the French infantry. In 1807, however, the continental block-

ade severely curtailed supplies of indigo dye to France, so a new uniform was designed, of a similar cut as before, of white with coloured regimental facings. Its issue, however, was limited, probably to the following regiments only: 3rd, 4th, 8th, 12th, 13th, 14th, 15th, 17th, 18th, 19th, 21st, 22nd, 23rd, 24th, 25th, 27th, 28th, 32nd, 33rd, 34th, 46th, 53rd and 86th. The white uniform proved highly unsatisfactory, and by 1808 the blue had been restored. Some units wore the white uniform in action, and one story attributes its withdrawal to the fact that Napoleon was sickened by the sight of bloodstained uniforms after the Battle of Eylau.

The 33rd Regiment (illustrated) wore violet facings. The shakos officially replaced the bicorn in 1806, though some had been worn earlier. Until sufficient French shakos had been manufactured, many captured Prussian ones were worn. The Grenadier companies (of which there was one per regiment) were distinguished by red plumes and shako ornaments and red epaulettes. The Voltigeurs (one company per regiment) wore these in yellow and green, while the ordinary Fusilier companies (usually six per regiment) wore cloth shoulder-straps and ball-pompoms on their shakos. The Quartermaster illustrated was distinguished by his gold chevrons, shako-cords, and 'crescents' on his epaulettes. At this time, some Grenadier companies retained the old bearskin cap.

Equipment was of the standard

French design: goatskin pack, grey or blue-grey overcoat, cartridge-box, sabre and bayonet. The white breeches and gaiters were often replaced by overalls on campaign, the white gaiters changing to black for wear in winter.

15. Holland: Private,
3rd Light Infantry, and
Officer, 2nd Infantry, c. 1807

In 1806, Napoleon's brother Louis was appointed King of Holland, succeeding the 'Grand Pensionary' Jan Schimmelpenninck who had ruled since the end of the revolutionary constitution of the Batavian Republic in 1805.

As was to be expected, the army of the new Kingdom of Holland was completely reorganised, and uniformed in the French pattern. Louis Bonaparte, however, refused to be intimidated by his brother, putting the interests of his new subjects before those of France. He even refused to introduce conscription, and as a result was forced to abdicate in 1810. The Netherlands and its army was then incorporated into the Empire, under direct control from Paris.

White was adopted as the national colour of the Kingdom of Holland in 1806, the style of the uniforms being greatly influenced by those of the French. The infantry were distinguished by coloured facings, different for each of the eight regiments, and by the regimental numbers on the shako. Grenadiers wore bearskin caps or

shakos with red feathers and red epaulettes, while those of the Voltigeurs were green. Light infantry regiments wore green uniforms and black leather equipment, as shown on the left-hand figure. These regiments were also distinguished by different facing colours.

In 1810 the army of the Kingdom of Holland was incorporated into that of France, the uniforms changing accordingly; only the Guard Regiment, which became the 3rd Grenadiers of the Imperial Guard, retained their old costume.

16. France: Mameluke trooper,
1806

On 13 October 1801, Bonaparte organised a troop of mamelukes, the warlike tribesmen he had fought in the Egyptian campaign, for French service. The nucleus of the troop was a band of about forty mamelukes he had brought from Egypt, the remainder being drawn from French cavalry regiments. The corps of mamelukes was attached to the Chasseurs à Cheval of the Imperial Guard, forming part of Napoleon's bodyguard.

The 'oriental' uniforms were basically alike in style, but as each man was allowed to wear whatever colour he chose, the appearance of the corps was quite startling. The headdress was a red 'tarboosh' worn with a white turban and, until about 1806, a brass plate on the front. The loose jacket and sleeveless waistcoat were worn in all shades of blue, green, red, crimson, yellow, white and brown, laced with a similar array of colours. Prior to about 1806–8, the jackets were collarless. The baggy trousers were usually white, brown, or various shades of red, and even the boots were often red, green or yellow.

Equipment was made in many colours, though white leather was the most common. Shabraques were usually green and sometimes bore the hunting-horn badge of the Chasseurs à Cheval. Harness was decorated with a large variety of embroidery, tassels, and even bells. Saddles were often oriental in style, with large brass stirrups. Officers' uniforms were similar to those of the other ranks, though even more colour-ful and grand. The mamelukes were not, however, mounted on Arab horses, but rode those of the Chasseurs à Cheval.

The weapons carried were even more varied than the uniforms; all manner of Turkish and Arabian sabres and scimitars, muskets, carbines, dag-gers, battle-axes and steel maces, all richly decorated. Pistols were carried tucked into the waist-sash or slung round the neck.

17. Spain: Villaviciosa Dragoons, Trooper, c. 1806

The Spanish army at the beginning of the nineteenth century was clothed and equipped in the late eighteenth-century manner which had already been abandoned by the rest of Europe.

Only when the Spanish army came under the influence of the French, and more importantly the British, were Spanish uniforms modernised.

In 1806 there were eight regiments of dragoons, all dressed in the tradi-tional lemon-yellow uniform first adopted in 1719. The regiments, listed in order of seniority, were distin-guished by coloured facings: Rey (crimson facings), Reina (light red), Almansa (light blue), Pavia (red facings, yellow collar), Villaviciosa (green), Sagunta (green facings, yellow collar), Numantia (black) and Lusitania (black facings, yellow collar). Lace and piping for all regiments was white (silver for officers, who also wore silver epaulettes), and each side of the collar bore an embroidered badge of a crossed sabre and palm leaf. The bicorn hats carried the red Spanish national cockade. Waistcoat and breeches were in the same colour as the coat, and white gaiters were worn under the riding-boots.

Equipment was in white leather, with black pouches. All ranks carried sabres and pistols, the rank and file being equipped with muskets and bayonets also. The cloaks, carried at the rear of the saddle, were yellow, with a falling collar in the facing colour.

18. Saxony: Guard Grenadiers. Privates, c. 1806

When the uniforms of the Saxon army were redesigned in 1810, one corps retained their old uniform. This was the 'Leib-Grenadier-Garde', or Guard Grenadier Regiment.

The headdress was the fur Grenadier cap common to many European armies, though of a distinctive pattern, the brass front plate being engraved with the 'F.A.R.' cipher of the King of Saxony, Friedrich Augustus. The cap had a yellow cloth patch at the rear, and was ornamented with white cords. The red coat was faced yellow, and all ranks wore epaulettes. After 1810, the breast of the coat was closed to the waist, so that the waistcoat was no longer visible.

Equipment was of white leather, the cross-belt having a brass match-case on the front, a relic of the days when matches were used for lighting hand grenades. Both ammunition pouches (one worn on the waistbelt) were made of black leather, and bore brass plates depicting the arms of Saxony.

Officers wore a similar uniform, but decorated with silver lace loops, of which there were nine on each lapel, two on each side of the collar, and two on each cuff, each loop of lace ending in a silver tassel. Officers also wore silver epaulettes and aiguillette on the right shoulder, and black knee-boots. The drum-major had an especially splendid costume, of yellow with dark blue facings and a profusion of silver lace, with red and white feather plumes in his bearskin cap.

19. France: Dragoons, c. 1812. Officers, 17th and 4th Regiments

There were thirty regiments of Dragoons in the French army at this period, of which the 1st, 3rd, 8th, 9th, 10th and 29th were converted to Chevau-Légers-Lanciers on 18 June 1811. There were regulations governing the uniforms of these corps, but they were often disregarded.

The brass helmet had its origin in the neo-classical style worn by the Voluntaires de Saxe in 1743, and was similar to that worn prior to the Revolution. The 'aigrette' or small tuft at the front and the falling 'mane' at the rear were of black horsehair; the helmet had a turban of brown fur or, very occasionally, of leopardskin like that worn by the Dragoons of the Imperial Guard. In full dress, plumes were worn on the left-hand side of the helmet; these were officially red (white for senior officers), though there were numerous regimental differences; for example, the 19th Regiment wore white plumes, the 3rd white with a red top and base, and other regiments frequently wore black plumes with the top in the facing colour, and sometimes with a green base. On campaign, the plumes were often replaced by a small pompom.

The coat was green, with open or, in the latter days of the Empire, closed lapels. The collar, cuffs, lapels, turn-backs and cuff-flaps were of the regimental facing colour, which was scarlet for the 1st to 6th Regiments, carmine for the 7th to 12th, pink for the 13th to 18th, yellow for the 19th to 24th, and light orange for the 25th to 30th. There were exceptions, however; green collars were worn by the 2nd, 5th, 8th, 11th, 14th, 17th, 20th, 23rd, 26th and 29th Regiments; green cuffs by the 3rd, 6th, 9th, 12th, 15th, 18th, 21st, 23rd, 24th, 27th and 30th; and green cuff-flaps by the 2nd, 5th, 8th, 11th, 17th, 20th, 23rd, 26th and 29th Regiments; and the 5th Regiment at some time wore green lapels. Officers wore silver epaulettes, and the other ranks had green shoulder-straps with piping of the facing colour, except for the 19th, who wore white epaulettes. In 1807–8 white epaulettes were also worn by the 2nd, 9th, 17th and 22nd Regiments. In full dress, white breeches were worn with black riding-boots, though on campaign grey breeches and on occasion overalls were used. For dismounted duty, the original function of the dragoons – that of mounted infantry – was recalled, for they wore black gaiters and carried bayonets with their carbines. In fact, there were several regiments of dismounted dragoons who acted as infantry during the Napoleonic Wars. The élite companies of dragoon regiments, the equivalent of the infantry grenadiers, often wore the bearskin cap with red plumes and cords, and red epaulettes.

Equipment was of white leather, with black pouches. Spurs were blackened for both officers and other ranks. The brass-hilted sabres had gold knots for officers, white for the rank and file, and white and red for the N.C.O.s. Greatcoats were green for officers and white for other ranks. The shabraques were green with silver lace edging for officers, and white lace edging for other ranks, who also had white sheepskin saddle-covers; officers had green holster-caps. Officers' shabraques bore an embroidered grenade badge in the rear corners, and the other ranks had the regimental number in the same place; but there were exceptions to this general rule.

20. Sweden: Royal Life Guard. Trooper and Officer, 1807

The Swedish Royal Life Guard (Konungens Lif Garde till Häst) had a strength of six squadrons, of which one squadron was dressed and equipped as Mounted Jägers.

The white uniform with pale blue facings shown on the right-hand figure was worn in full dress; on active service the pale blue uniform of the left-hand figure was often adopted. The lace on both uniforms was silver for officers and white for other ranks. The yellow-barrelled sash worn by the Life Guard was that adopted for all Swedish dragoon regiments in 1795. The sabretache, adopted by all· the Swedish cavalry in 1795, bore the three gold crowns of the Swedish Royal Arms. Officers of the Life Guard wore the white 'brassard', common to all

Swedish officers, on the left arm, as a commemoration of the Palace Revolution of 1772. The Mounted Jäger troop wore a uniform cut in a similar style, but of dark green, with black leather equipment in place of the white of the other troops.

The most noteworthy feature of the uniform was the headdress, the characteristically Swedish 'kusket', a black 'round hat' with a turned-up brim, fitted with a bearskin crest and ornamented with cords. The light blue and yellow Swedish cockade was worn at the base of the plume. In 1813, in common with many Swedish regiments, the 'kusket' was replaced by a black shako.

21. Denmark: King's Life Rifle Corps. Rifleman and Officer in full dress, 1807

The King's Life Rifle Corps (Kongens Livjäger Corps) was a volunteer regiment formed from members of the upper middle class in Copenhagen in 1801, to combat the threat of Admiral Parker's fleet which was reported off the coast of Denmark. The original strength was two companies, though this was increased to four, of 100 men each, after the Battle of Copenhagen. Officers were elected by the riflemen. The regiment earned its great reputation in 1807, when it lost over a quarter of its men in the unsuccessful defence of Copenhagen against the British attack.

The uniform shown is that introduced by the Regulations of 1806. The jacket was dark green with black facings and braid; gold lace was worn by the officers in full dress, though in service dress their uniform was like that of the men, with gold epaulettes to distinguish their rank. Hessian boots were worn by all ranks, and officers were allowed green pelisses with black fur edging, as an optional extra to their uniform.

The headdress was the most remarkable feature of the uniform, being a variation of the czapka, with parallel sides and a green cloth turban. Cords were green for riflemen, gold for officers, and white for N.C.O.s, who were also distinguished by a gold epaulette on the right shoulder. Officers wore gold and crimson sashes in service dress, and were allowed sword-knots of the regular army pattern, of gold with two crimson stripes, a privilege not normally extended to volunteer corps.

Prior to 1806, officers' epaulettes were green, and their sashes (worn only in service dress) were green and yellow; they adopted czapkas like the riflemen in 1806, wearing British-style 'Tarleton' helmets until that date.

All ranks, including officers, were armed with rifled muskets, which were provided by the government; all other clothing and equipment was provided by the riflemen themselves. Equipment and pouches were of black leather, and powder flasks were carried by all ranks in service dress.

22. Sweden: Life Grenadier Regiment and Grenadier Corps of the Life Brigade. Officers, c. 1813

This plate depicts the uniform of two of the Swedish Grenadier regiments in 1813.

The Life Grenadier Regiment wore the dark blue single-breasted infantry jacket which had replaced the previous grey uniform in 1810. The facings were red, with white lace (silver for officers). The headdress, the Swedish 'kusket', had a bearskin crest placed at an oblique angle across the top of the hat. The crest was later altered to run from front to rear, and later still from side to side. The officer is shown wearing a waistbelt, fastened with a plate bearing the Swedish Royal Arms, but other ranks wore a broad Lancer-style girdle, of yellow with two blue horizontal stripes.

The Grenadier Corps of the Life Brigade was formed in 1808 from the Light Infantry of the Life Brigade. A similar style of uniform to the Life Grenadier Regiment was worn, with white facings; the yellow lace (gold for officers) was introduced in 1813–14. All ranks wore epaulettes, gold for officers and yellow for the rank and file. Blue and yellow girdles were worn by the other ranks, who also carried a sabre, suspended from the white crossbelts. Musket-slings were orange-red. The corps included a company of Jägers, who wore a similar uniform, with black belts, green plumes and green sword-knots. The crest on the 'kusket' ran from front to rear; the brass band round the headdress was officially discontinued in 1810, but in many cases continued to be worn. Both Grenadier regiments wore a brass grenade badge on the front of the 'kusket' in addition to the brass band.

23. Italy: Guard of Honour. Troopers, Bologna, Rome and Milan companies, c. 1808

24/25. Italy: Guard of Honour. Officers and Trooper, c. 1808

The Kingdom of Italy was formed in 1805 by Napoleon, who crowned himself as King, and appointed his stepson, Eugène de Beauharnais, as Viceroy. The army was extended to include the appropriate Royal Guard, of which the senior corps was the Guard of Honour, a regiment of heavy cavalry.

The Guard of Honour originally consisted of four companies, each company being drawn from a specific district, and each having a different facing colour: 1st Company (Milan) pink; 2nd (Bologna) yellow; 3rd (Brescia) chamois; 4th (Rome) scarlet. In 1808 a fifth company, from Venice, was added, this having orange facings. All members of the Guard were drawn from wealthy and aristocratic families, each man being awarded a commission after two years' service. The corps had a 'double rank' system, whereby officers of the Guard ranked one higher than other regiments; e.g. a Major in the Guard was the equivalent of a Lieutenant-Colonel of another regiment. This system was not unique, being used in the British Foot Guards also. The Guard fought, and suffered heavy losses, in the Russian campaign of 1812.

The uniform was of the traditional Italian green, styled like that of the French dragoons. The gilt helmets were surmounted by a large eagle, which supported the black bearskin crest. The lower part of the helmet was bound in white metal, this bearing the letter 'N' under a representation of the ancient Iron Crown of Lombardy, which Napoleon had used in his coronation. The Crown was also borne on the sword-guard, and on the breast of the Italian eagle badge which ornamented the pouch. Officers were distinguished by silver lace and epaulettes; their aiguillettes were silver, those of the other ranks being white.

The undress uniform is shown in Plates 24/25; single-breasted green jackets were worn, devoid of facings, with green forage caps, those of the officers being ornamented with silver lace, and those of the rank and file by bands of the facing colour. The officer wearing the greatcoat in Plate 24/25 is wearing loose overalls with black leather to the knees in imitation of boots, a style favoured by the French general Lasalle. On active service grey overalls were worn, these being 'strapped' (lined on the inside leg) with black leather. Greatcoats were green, and cloaks were white, the latter being lined with the facing colour.

26. Spain: Guerrillas, c. 1809

Early in 1808, Napoleon occupied Spain with about 100,000 men. Though the Spanish government was under French control, the population of Madrid bitterly resented the army of occupation, and rose in rebellion on 2 May. Thirty-one French were killed, and savage reprisals and executions followed. After the rising, Napoleon appointed his brother Joseph as King of Spain, which was the signal for a general revolt throughout Spain.

In the Peninsular War which followed, Napoleon lost an average of 100 men per day as bands of 'guerrillas', varying in strength from a handful to the size of a small army, ravaged his lines of communication. These bands, composed of peasants, volunteers and militiamen, murdered and raided to such a degree that, in effect, two French armies were needed in Spain, one to oppose Wellington, and one to protect the French rear from the guerrillas. It was this constant drain on manpower and resources which brought about the eventual downfall of Napoleon.

Wellington wrote of the guerrillas that 'when inflamed, there is no violence or outrage they do not commit . . . the Spaniard is an undisciplined savage . . .'. Indeed, the guerrillas war was a ghastly catalogue of horror and brutality, fearful atrocities being committed by both sides, portrayed by Goya in his 'Disasters of War'. Like the ordinary guerrillas, their leaders came from all walks of life; one was a priest who claimed to have personally killed 600 Frenchmen; Martin Diez, known as El Empecinado, a labourer's son who once captured Guadalajara; Mina, a student; and the savage Don Julian Sanchez, who vowed to slice Marshal Soult into strips if ever he caught the Frenchman!

Guerrilla costume was predominantly civilian, though items of uniform were worn at every opportunity; clothing captured from the French and supplied by the British was mixed with their own fantastic designs of shakos, 'round hats', and, in the case of some of the officers, even dolmans and pelisses. Weapons were of every conceivable variety, captured, British-supplied or home-made. There was little attempt to differentiate guerrilla bands by uniform, though those of Catalonia favoured blue jackets with red facings (illustrated is a private of the Catalonian Caçadores, wearing an elaborate shako), yellow with black braid for the Chispero Madrileno, and yellow for the Valencia Volunteers.

27. France: Chasseurs à Cheval of the Imperial Guard. Trooper, full dress, 1808

In the campaigns in Italy and Egypt, Napoleon had formed a corps of light cavalry to act as his bodyguard, the 'Guides du Général Bonaparte'. On 2 December 1799, the Guides from the Egyptian campaign were incorporated into the Consular Guard as a troop of Chasseurs à Cheval, 112 strong, and commanded by Eugène de Beauharnais. When Napoleon became Emperor, the Consular Guard became the Imperial Guard, and the Chasseurs à Cheval were increased in strength, becoming Napoleon's official escort.

The regiment, nicknamed 'The Invincibles', served with distinction in every one of Napoleon's campaigns, a squadron being in constant attendance on the Emperor. The uniform most often worn by Napoleon was the undress 'surtout' of the Chasseurs à Cheval, worn under his familiar grey overcoat; Marshal Bessières, the original commander of the Guides in 1796, and later commander of the cavalry of the Imperial Guard, also favoured the uniform of the regiment. Disbanded in 1814, the corps was briefly re-formed in 1815, to act as Napoleon's escort during the 'Hundred Days' campaign, before final disbandment on 26 October 1815.

The uniform was predominantly hussar-style, green dolmans and scarlet pelisses being worn in full dress. On campaign, the buckskin breeches were replaced by green or grey overalls with orange or red stripes down the outside leg. On active service the pelisse was occasionally worn as a coat, but the more common service dress consisted of the green undress 'surtout' coat which had scarlet collar and cuffs and orange piping. A scarlet waistcoat with orange braid was also worn. On active service, the fur busby or 'colpack' was sometimes covered with black oilskin, and the full dress sabre-tache (as illustrated) was replaced by one of black leather which bore the Imperial Arms in brass. Barrelled sashes were red and green. The rank and file were armed with carbines and bayonets in addition to the sabres and pistols which were carried by all ranks.

Officers were distinguished by a profusion of gold lace on the uniform, green pouch-belts with gold lace, green and gold barrelled sashes, red harness with gilt fittings, and leopardskin shabraques. Senior officers had white plumes. With parade dress, officers wore scarlet breeches.

28. Württemberg: Garde Jäger Squadron. Officer, c. 1808

The state of Württemberg was part of the Confederation of the Rhine, thus being allied to Napoleon until after the defeat of the French at Leipzig, when the King of Württemberg changed sides, his army then forming part of the allied forces.

The ancient corps of Guard cavalry of Württemberg consisted, at the time of the Confederation of the Rhine, of four squadrons, each wearing a different costume; the Garde du Corps, who wore yellow with black facings; two squadrons of Horse Grenadiers, who wore a uniform like that of the French Grenadiers à Cheval of the Imperial Guard, of blue with yellow facings; and the senior corps of the Guard cavalry,

the squadron of Mounted Jägers, who wore the green uniform with black facings illustrated.

The helmet worn by the Garde Jägers was like that worn by the Württemberg cavalry, of black leather with a woollen crest, the pierced gilt front plate consisting of the Royal Arms of Württemberg. Over the jacket was worn the black 'supreveste' common to many European Royal Bodyguards, being worn in the Russian and Imperial German armies until the outbreak of the First World War. The 'supreveste' of the officers of the Württemberg Garde Jägers was edged with gold lace, those of the other ranks being edged in a chequered design of black and yellow. Both the front and back of the 'supreveste' of all ranks was decorated with a representation of the Star of the Military Service Order of Württemberg. The waist sash worn by officers was silver, with red and gold strands throughout. The cipher of the King of Württemberg was borne on the holstercaps.

In 1810 the headdress was changed to that of a Grenadier cap, as worn by the Horse Grenadier squadrons of the Guard cavalry, but with a large green plume on the left-hand side.

29. Prussia: 2nd Life Hussars. Trooper and Officer, c. 1809

Following the defeat at Jena and Auerstadt in October 1805, the Prussian army was reorganised. In 1808 the

Leib (Life) Hussars were formed from the Prittwitz provisional hussar regiment, the remnants of Von Prittwitz's 5th Hussars which was originally raised in 1741 as the 'Black Hussars'. On 20 December 1808 the new Life Hussar Regiment was divided into two units, the 1st and 2nd Life Hussars, which ranked as the senior Hussar regiments in the Prussian army. In 1812 the regiments furnished two squadrons each to form the 1st Combined Hussars of Marshal Macdonald's 10th Corps of Napoleon's Grande Armée. The first officer to be awarded the Legion of Honour for the Russian campaign was reputedly a member of the Combined Hussars. In 1813–14 campaign the two Life Hussar regiments were again in action, this time against Napoleon, after Prussia had changed her allegiance.

The regiments wore uniforms of the typical hussar style, with dolmans and pelisses of the unusual black colour. This, together with the Death's Head badge on the shako, created a very ominous, though striking, appearance. The Death's Head badge was a feature of certain Prussian uniforms as early as the 1740s, and lasted until the days of the Nazi defeat. Until about 1809 the Death's Head on the shako of the Life Hussars was made of white cloth; afterwards it was made of metal. Facings were red for both regiments, the only distinguishing feature being the shoulder-straps on both the pelisse and dolman, which were white for the 1st Regiment and red for the 2nd. On campaign, grey overalls, with red stripes down the outside leg of those of the officers, were worn, and the shakos were enclosed in black oilskin covers, sometimes bearing the Death's Head badge. Lace was silver for officers and white for other ranks; the pelisses were lined with scarlet. The pouch bore the 'Garde Star', a representation of the Star of the Order of the Black Eagle. In full dress, sabretaches were red with white lace (silver for officers), bearing the crowned 'FWR' cipher of the King of Prussia. Troopers were armed with carbines in addition to the sabre, which was carried by all ranks.

The regiment included a squadron of Mounted Jägers, whose uniform was identical to that of the Hussar squadrons, but of dark green with red facings and shoulder-straps, green and black barrelled sashes, and green overalls, reinforced with black leather around the bottom and on the inside leg, with black stripes down the outer seam. Officers of the Jäger squadron frequently wore the dolman open, to display their elegant light blue waistcoat, which was heavily braided in gold.

30. Portugal: Caçadores. Atirador Corporal, 4th Battalion, and Private, 5th Battalion, 1808

Until 1808 the Portuguese army contained no light infantry. In October of that year, six battalions of riflemen or 'Caçadores' were raised, each with a strength of 628 men; each battalion consisted of five companies, including one of 'atiradores' or sharpshooters. Their organisation was based upon that of the British rifle regiments, and their purpose was to combat the French 'Voltigeurs' by forming a skirmishing corps for Wellington's Anglo-Portuguese army. Largely commanded by British officers, the Caçadores performed magnificently throughout the Peninsular War, fighting alongside the British riflemen, and contributing greatly to the French defeat.

The uniform depicted only lasted until the regulations of July 1809. The false-fronted shako was of the 'Barretina' pattern worn by all the Portuguese infantry. The number of the battalion was borne in the loop of the bugle-horn badge on the brass plate. High on the front of the cap was a small brass oval bearing the arms of Portugal. Plumes were black for the 'atirador' companies, and green for the remainder.

The British-style jackets were brown, with different facings for each battalion: 1st, brown collar with sky-blue cuffs; 2nd, brown with red cuffs; 3rd, brown with yellow cuffs; 4th, sky blue; 5th, red; 6th, yellow. Lace was gold for officers and yellow for other ranks; officers and sergeants wore 'scaled' epaulettes with gold and yellow fringes respectively, the rank and file having brown 'wings' with green braid, and green fringes for the atiradores. Officers were further distinguished by crimson waist sashes, Hussar boots, and gilt gorgets which bore the Portuguese arms in silver. As illustrated, cor-

porals wore bands of lace around the top of the cuffs. The white breeches and black gaiters were replaced on campaign by brown breeches and black half-gaiters with green braid around the top. All ranks carried brass-hilted swords, and at this early part of the corps' existence, the rank and file were armed with regulation infantry muskets, though these were later replaced by carbines.

In 1809 the uniform changed, 'stovepipe' shakos replacing the 'Barretina' pattern, and black facings, black 'wings' and black hussar-style braiding being adopted for the jackets of all battalions. In 1811, six more battalions were raised, and coloured facings were restored on the following pattern: 1st Battalion, black collar with light blue cuffs; 2nd, black with scarlet cuffs; 3rd, black; 4th, light blue; 5th, scarlet; 6th, yellow; 7th, black with yellow cuffs; 8th, light blue with black cuffs; 9th, scarlet with black cuffs; 10th, yellow with black cuffs; 11th, light blue with scarlet cuffs; 12th, scarlet with light blue cuffs.

31. Prussia: General Staff.
'Flügel-Adjutant', 1808;
King's Adjutant-General,
Cavalry, 1808;
Aide-de-Camp, Cavalry, 1812

The uniform of the Prussian General Staff varied according to rank. The most common uniform for General Officers was a dark blue coatee with scarlet facings and gold oak-leaf lace.

Junior Staff officers, however, wore the uniforms illustrated. The left-hand figure, a 'Flügel-Adjutant', wore an infantry coatee with silver lace on the collar and cuffs in the style of the Foot Guard Regiments, with a silver aiguillette suspended from the right shoulder. The shako was of the 1808 pattern, bearing the silver and white Prussian cockade on the front. A unique feature of the headdress was the silver chain looped round the body, held by two small eagles at either side of the shako; this chain could also be used as a chinstrap.

Cavalry officers occupying positions on the staff were allowed to wear bicorn hats and the white cavalry 'Kollet' (coatee) with appropriate facings. The central figure is one of the King's Adjutant-Generals, distinguished by the scarlet facings of the Kollet and the gold aiguillette on the right shoulder. Aides-de-camp, whose uniform is shown on the right-hand figure, wore the same Kollet with facings of bright green velvet, these being adopted at the end of 1812. Prior to that date, green piping alone distinguished their uniforms.

All officers wore the waist-sash in the national colours of silver and black, which were repeated in the design of the plumes. In full dress a black and silver cockade and golden loop were worn on the right-hand side of the bicorn. Grey overalls were worn on campaign, when the shakos were often covered with black oilskin. Swords were usually of infantry pattern, though cavalry sabres were sometimes carried.

In 1814 the white uniform was abolished, when all staff officers adopted the dark blue uniform, the style of which was altered, the cuffs becoming pointed and the collar being closed, both laced with gold. Officers of the General Staff and War Ministry wore the uniform of a 'Flügel-Adjutant', with crimson facings.

32. Austria: Hungarian Grenadiers, 1814. Officers and Private.

In 1814 the Austrian army was composed of 'German' and 'Hungarian' regiments, thirteen regiments of infantry being drawn from the Imperial province of Hungary. These regiments and their titles are listed below, together with their facing colours: 2nd Alexander IV Russland (yellow), 19th Hesse Homburg (light blue), 32nd Nikolaus Esterhazy (light blue), 33rd H. Colloredomansfeld (dark blue), 34th Paul Daidovitz (madder red), 37th Andreas Marriassy (bright red), 48th Josef Simbschen (steel green), 51st Gabriel Spleny (dark blue), 52nd Erzherzog Franz Carl (dark red), 53rd Joh. Jellachich (dark red), 60th Ignaz Gyulai (steel green), 61st St. Julien (grass green), 62nd Theoror Wocquant (grass green).

The uniform of these regiments conformed to those of the rest of the Austrian infantry, though with some Hungarian distinctions. The white coat had pointed cuffs instead of the 'round' cuffs of the 'German' regiments. These pointed cuffs bore a lace ornament or 'Barentatzen'. 'Hungarian' regiments wore tight-fitting sky-blue breeches with yellow and black braid and short black gaiters, instead of the white breeches and black knee-gaiters of the 'German' regiments.

The fur cap worn by the Grenadier companies was like that of the rest of the Austrian infantry, bearing the Imperial arms on the brass front plate. The bag at the rear is generally depicted in contemporary pictures as being of the facing colour, with blue 'zigzag' lines. A spray of oakleaves was worn behind the black and yellow cockade. In campaign dress the cap was often covered with a black oilskin. Officers' lace was in gold or silver, and their sashes were gold with black strands.

Equipment was of white leather, the rank and file carrying a calfskin pack, upon which was strapped the dark grey overcoat, and a brass-hilted sabre. Grenadier officers of the Austrian army often carried curved sabres and sometimes pistols, carried in holsters suspended from a shoulder-belt.

33. Saxe–Coburg–Saalfeld Infantry. Privates, 1809

In 1806, the small Saxon duchies of Saxe–Coburg–Saalfeld, Saxe–Gotha–Altenburg, Saxe–Hildburghausen, Saxe–Meiningen and Saxe–Weimar were required, by the agreement of 15 December 1806, to provide a contingent for the army of the Confederation of the Rhine. Together, the states raised a troop of 40 hussars and 2,800 infantry.

Duke Ernest of Saxe–Coburg–Saalfeld (whose son Albert was to become the consort of Queen Victoria) raised a battalion of infantry, the 'Battalion Coburg–Saalfeld', which formed part of the 4th Regiment of the Confederation army. The uniform of this battalion was a mixture of French and German styles. The shako was French, and had a brass diamond-shaped plate which bore the cipher of the Duke. Hungarian-style breeches with yellow Austrian knots and side stripes were worn in full dress, with black cloth gaiters cut to resemble knee boots; on campaign, either light blue or brown overalls were worn. Officers wore bicorn hats, and the Grenadier company was distinguished by fur caps with red plumes, and red epaulettes. Equipment and sidearms were like those of the French army.

The battalion fought in the Peninsular War, and was present at the Siege of Gerona in 1809. This city and its Spanish garrison was besieged for seven months, until the Governor, Mariano Alvarez, and the entire garrison were prostrate from exhaustion and sickness. By 10 December 1809, when the Spanish surrendered, 20,000 French and allied casualties had been incurred by the stubborn defence of the city. The entire population fought in this heroic siege, including even the monks, who formed themselves into a volunteer company called 'The Crusaders', and helped to man the walls. It was the most glorious chapter in the history of the Spanish army in the entire war.

34. Russia: Jäger Officers, 1809

Russian Jäger regiments were composed, like the other Russian infantry, of three battalions. Each battalion was composed of three companies of Jägers and one of Jäger-grenadiers. The Jäger-grenadier company comprised one platoon of Jäger-grenadiers and one platoon of carabiniers.

The uniform of the Jäger regiments closely followed the Russian infantry pattern. The shako, which had been introduced in 1803-5, was adopted by the Jägers in 1807; prior to that date they had worn felt 'round hats'. In 1809 the white caplines (silver for officers) were added. The shako bore the Russian cockade of black, silver and orange, and a silver pompom with an orange centre which bore the Imperial cipher. For other ranks, the pompom was white with the centre in the colour of the individual company. Bicorn hats were also worn by officers in some orders of dress.

The jacket was like that of the remainder of the Russian infantry, but with green facings and red piping. Prior to 1807, the uniform colour was a lighter green than the rest of the infantry, but in that year the regulation dark green was adopted. The epaulettes bore the number of the division to which the regiment was attached. Officers wore silver and gilt gorgets bearing the Imperial cipher, suspended from orange cords, and the regulation sashes of silver with orange strands. The breeches were also dark green, though white ones were worn in summer, with black gaiters. Officers' greatcoats were dark green with red piping; those of the other ranks were brown. When wearing the greatcoat, the officers' swords were worn underneath, with only the hilt protruding from the left-hand pocket.

Equipment was in black leather; the cartridge boxes of the rank and file bore the regimental number in brass numerals.

35. France: Portuguese Legion. Officers of Cavalry and Infantry, c. 1809

In January 1808, a corps of Portuguese troops was authorised to be raised for French service. By 18 May 1808 the Portuguese Legion comprised six regiments of infantry, two regiments of light cavalry, and a battery of artillery. In May 1811 the Legion was re-organised into three regiments of infantry and one of light cavalry, and the whole corps was disbanded in November 1813, after serving with distinction at Wagram (1809) and in the Russian campaign of 1812.

Both infantry and cavalry wore brown uniforms with red facings and white piping, cut in the French style, as illustrated. Officers wore gold epaulettes; infantry rank and file had brown shoulder-straps with red piping. Grenadiers were distinguished by red epaulettes, and Voltigeurs by green epaulettes with red 'crescents'. Infantry officers wore either bicorn hats, or shakos like those of the men, which were of the false-fronted 'Barretina' type, as worn by the Portuguese army, with brass plates. Grenadiers wore red plumes and cords on their shakos, and Voltigeurs green cords and yellow plumes with red bases, as illustrated. White breeches and black gaiters, or white trousers with red piping were worn by the infantry. Greatcoats were brown, and officers were distinguished by red waist sashes and gilt gorgets.

The cavalry troopers wore similar jackets to the infantry, but with red woollen 'wings', and light blue breeches with red lace and Austrian knots (gold lace for officers). Their black leather helmets were fitted with brass, and surmounted by a black woollen crest. Red plumes were worn by all ranks of the cavalry except by senior officers, who wore white feathers. The shabraques of the cavalry troopers were white sheepskin, with a red 'wolf's tooth' edge. Officers' shabraques were originally brown with gold lace, though these changed to red with silver lace. Equipment and weapons for both infantry and cavalry were of French pattern.

About 1811 the uniform of the cavalry was redesigned in the pattern of the French Chasseurs à Cheval, though the brown colour was retained. Officers' lace became silver instead of gold.

36. France: Geographical Engineers, c. 1809

In 1796 a French engineer officer, Louis-Albert-Guillain Bacler d'Albe (1761–1824) was appointed Geographer to the Army of Italy, with responsibility to map the area over which the French army was to fight. So well did he complete the task that in 1804 he was appointed head of the Topographical Bureau, and from then until 1813 was constantly in attendance at Napoleon's side. Bacler d'Albe, eventually promoted to General, was undoubtedly a considerable help to the Emperor in the planning and execution of his campaigns. His Topographical Department, with a staff of one hundred officers, was perhaps the most vital part of the Imperial Staff, mapping the routes of the French army.

The uniform of the Geographical Engineer officers was basically of the dark blue infantry pattern, consisting of the simple 'surtout' with only the collar in the facing colour, originally sky blue but later changed to dull orange. The epaulettes and buttons were gilt. Breeches were like those of the infantry, white or dark blue in winter, worn with riding-boots which had turndown tops. The bicorn, of the universal pattern, was also like that of the infantry officers.

37. Bavaria: Infantry. Sharpshooter, Preysing Regiment; Grenadier, Leib Regiment; 1809

The contribution of the Elector of Bavaria, Maximilian Joseph, to the Confederation of the Rhine, which he joined in 1806, was an army of 30,000 men.

The headdress of the Bavarian infantry was the 'Raupenhelm' or crested helmet, which was worn until 1885. This black leather helmet was fitted with brass ornaments, the front plate bearing the Royal 'MJ' cipher. The crest was made of bearskin for officers and wool for other ranks. On the left-hand side of the helmet was the Bavarian national cockade of light blue and white, over which the Grenadier companies wore a red plume, and sharpshooters a green plume. Grenadier companies of the second battalions of infantry regiments had red over white plumes.

Jackets were of the traditional light blue, used by the Bavarian army from the time of the Seven Years War until 1918. Each regiment had facings of a different colour, those of the Preysing Regiment being pink. In some orders of dress, white gaiters replaced the black ones illustrated. Officers were distinguished by silver lace, and silver waist sashes with light blue vertical strands. Equipment was white leather, with fawn packs and black leather cartridge pouches. Greatcoats were grey.

The Leib Regiment, the senior corps of the Bavarian infantry, wore a similar uniform, but with red facings and white lace loops on the breast and cuffs. The Grenadier company, as illustrated, wore bearskin caps with the plume in the national colours of light blue and white. At the rear of the cap was a scarlet cloth patch bearing a white cross.

38. Prussia: Garde Jäger Battalion, 1809. Private and Officer

After the defeat of 1806, the Feldjäger Regiment of the Prussian army was reduced to two companies. After the Peace of Tilsit the strength had increased to nine companies, which in 1808 were reorganised into two battalions, the Garde Jäger Battalion and the East Prussian Jäger Battalion. A third corps of riflemen, the Silesian Schützen Battalion, was raised in 1809.

The uniform of the Garde Jägers was similar in style to the other Prussian infantry regiments. The shakos carried as a badge the Star of the Order of the Black Eagle, in brass for the rank and file and in silver, gilt and enamel for officers. The large black feather plumes and green cords (silver for officers) were reserved for full dress; on active service, the shakos were covered with black oilskin. The shakos also bore the black and white national cockade; the chain chinstrap of the officers was supported by two small gilt eagles on either side of the shako.

The 'Kollet' or jacket, green instead

of the usual blue, had red facings and bore the yellow lace loops (gold for officers) which distinguished the Garde regiments. The officers wore the regulation silver sash with black strands. Breeches were grey, and always worn with black knee-boots, though officers wore grey overalls. Equipment was black leather, the cartridge pouches bearing the Star of the Order of the Black Eagle in brass. On the front of the crossbelt, riflemen carried a small powderflask. Officers were armed with curved sabres; other ranks had short, brass-hilted swords. Sword-knots were silver and black for officers, silver and green for N.C.O.s, and green for riflemen.

The East Prussian Jägers were similarly uniformed, though without the lace on the 'Kollet', and with a shako badge of a large Prussian cockade. The Silesian Schützen Battalion had black facings with red piping, green cuff-flaps, and no shako cords, but otherwise were dressed like the East Prussian corps. When, in 1814, the Garde Schützen Battalion was raised, their uniform was like that of the Silesian Battalion, but with the addition of the Garde lace and the star shako badge.

39. Austria: 7th Regiment ('F.M.L. Baron Schröder') of Infantry, 1809. Officer and Private of Grenadiers

The 'German' regiments of the Austrian army wore the traditional white uniform shown in Plate 31, but with 'round' cuffs, and white breeches. Until 1806, black leather helmets with black over yellow woollen crests (introduced in 1798) were worn by the ordinary companies of infantry battalions, until the shako was adopted in that year. The Grenadier companies, however, retained their bearskin caps.

Below is a list of the sixty-four infantry regiments in the Imperial army in 1809, together with their nationality, facing colour and colour of buttons (yellow or white):

1	German	Light rose	Y
2	German	Deep yellow	Y
3	German	Sky blue	W
4	German	Sky blue	Y
5	German	Dark blue	W
6	German	Black	W
7	German	Dark blue	W
8	German	Wine red	Y
9	Walloon	Apple green	Y
10	German	Light green	W
11	German	Rose red	W
12	German	Dark brown	Y
13	German	Green	Y
14	German	Black	Y
15	German	Madder	Y
16	German	Violet	Y
17	German	Pale brown	W
18	German	Pale rose	W
19	Hungarian	Sky blue	W
20	German	Red	W
21	German	Sea green	Y
22	German	Deep yellow	W
23	German	Wine red	W
24	German	Dark blue	W
25	German	Sea green	W

26	German	Light green	Y
27	German	Deep yellow	Y
28	German	Grass green	W
29	German	Medium blue	W
30	Walloon	Light blue	Y
31	German	Deep yellow	W
32	Hungarian	Sky blue	Y
33	Hungarian	Deep blue	W
34	Hungarian	Madder	W
35	German	Red	Y
36	German	Pale grey	W
37	Hungarian	Wine red	Y
38	Hungarian	Rose red	Y
39	Hungarian	Wine red	W
40	German	Crimson	W
41	German	Lemon yellow	W
42	German	Orange	W
43	German	Lemon yellow	W
44	Italian	Madder	W
45	German	Crimson	Y
46	German	Dark blue	Y
47	German	Grey green	W
48	Hungarian	Grey green	Y
49	German	Pale grey	W
50	German	Violet	W
51	German	Dark blue	Y
52	Hungarian	Pale rose	Y
53	Croat	Pale rose	W
54	Croat	Apple green	W
55	Walloon	Medium blue	Y
56	German	Grey green	Y
57	German	Pale grey	Y
58	Walloon	Black	W
59	German	Orange	Y
60	Hungarian	Grey green	W
61	Hungarian	Grass green	Y
62	Hungarian	Grass green	W
63	Walloon	Deep green	W
64	German	Medium grey	—

40/41. Britain: Infantry and General Staff, 1809. Officer, Light Company, 14th Foot; Private, 43rd Light Infantry; General Officer; Officer, 4th Foot

There were two types of light infantry in the British army; each ordinary infantry battalion included a company of light troops, and there were six 'specialist' light regiments, the 43rd, 51st, 52nd, 68th, 71st and 85th. The duty of both types of light infantry was to act as skirmishers, the 'Light Division' of the Peninsular War (comprising the 43rd and 52nd Light Infantry and the 95th Rifles) being perhaps the most famous, and certainly the most successful, formation in the whole of Europe.

The first two figures show the uniform of the light infantry. The shako, similar to the 'stove-pipe' of the line infantry, bore the green plume and bugle-horn badge of the light infantry. The red jacket (scarlet for officers) was the same in style as those of the ordinary infantry, the regimental distinctions being in the colour of the facings and the colour and arrangement of the lace. The facings of the 14th (Buckinghamshire) Regiment were buff, and those of the 43rd (Monmouthshire) Light Infantry white. The lace was silver or gold (silver for the 14th) for officers, and white with a coloured pattern for other ranks (that of the 43rd having a pattern of red and black lines, and worn in pairs). The 'wings' on the jacket were a distinction of the 'flank' companies (light infantry and grenadiers), those of the officers being in scales or chains. The sash with looped cords was also a feature peculiar to light infantry and rifle regiments. Officers' breeches (buff for the 14th) were worn with boots or gaiters; the white breeches and black knee-gaiters of the other ranks were replaced on campaign with grey overalls and short gaiters, though for a time the 43rd wore white overalls. The equipment was of the regulation white leather, the regiments being distinguished by the design of their shoulder-belt plates. Canteens were carried on brown leather straps. The curved sabre illustrated was exclusive to officers of 'flank' companies, light infantry and rifles.

The right-hand figure shows an officer of the 4th (King's Own) Regiment, in the long-skirted coat of the line infantry, which was replaced by the jacket in 1812. The facings of the 4th were dark blue, with gold lace. The officers' lapels were sometimes worn turned back to display the facing colour, as illustrated. The epaulette and sash were distinguishing features of the 'Battalion companies'; the bicorn hat was worn by all infantry officers (except light infantry and rifles) until they adopted the 'Belgic' shako upon its introduction in 1812. Battalion company officers carried straight-bladed swords with gilt hilts and gold and crimson sword-knots. Both officers are

shown in campaign dress, with canteens and blanket-roll.

The mounted figure is a General Officer, wearing the regulation scarlet coat with blue facings and gold lace, cut in a style basically like that of the infantry. The bicorn hat was worn by the staff throughout the Napoleonic period. The officer illustrated is carrying a stirrup-hilted light cavalry sabre, though numerous variations of sword were carried by staff officers.

42. The Brunswick Corps. Jäger and Infantry privates, 1809

In April 1809 the dispossessed Duke of Brunswick–Oels and Lüneburg, Frederick William, raised a 2,000-strong 'free corps' of infantry and cavalry in Bohemia, which he placed at the service of Austria. In June 1809, together with 7,500 Austrians, the Brunswick Corps invaded Saxony, but after the Austrian defeat at Wagram, Frederick William marched his corps into Westphalia, causing havoc and defeating the enemy on several occasions. When surrounded by overwhelming numbers, the Duke cut his way out and was evacuated from Elsfleth by the British fleet. Being landed at Yarmouth and Grimsby, the corps entered British service on 14 August 1809.

From there, the Brunswick Corps – consisting of infantry, jägers and a troop of hussars – served with the British army in the Peninsular War.

Originally of very fine material, the quality of the corps declined rapidly when Croats, Italians, Poles, Dutch and Danish were drafted in, until its discipline and desertion rate was the worst of any British corps in the war. However, it was a greatly experienced unit, and on occasion distinguished itself in action. In 1813 the corps was enlarged to include Lancers and Artillery, into the Brunswick Legion, which served in the 'Hundred Days' campaign, Frederick William being killed at Quatre Bras.

The uniform of the Jäger companies, green with red facings, was similar to that of the Prussian army, with an Austrian-style 'round hat' with a turned-up brim. The Jägers were armed with rifled muskets and side-arms in the style of hunting swords. The infantry uniform was sombre in the extreme; Lady de Lancey described the Brunswick Corps as 'an immense moving hearse'. The entire uniform was black, relieved only by the sky-blue facings and the white metal skull and crossed bones on the shako, which also had a large 'falling' plume of black horsehair. The coat was a knee-length, Polish-style 'polrock' with black braid, fastened by black, cloth-covered toggles. All equipment was of black leather, except for the brown calfskin pack. Officers were distinguished by silver sashes and sabres.

The uniform of the Hussars consisted of a black dolman and breeches, with a shako similar to that worn by the infantry. The Lancers were originally dressed in green Austrian-style uniforms, but later they adopted the black of the remainder of the corps. When the Brunswick Legion was formed, the 'polrock' was retained by only the Leib-Battalion, the other six infantry regiments being clothed in black jackets.

43. France: 1st Chasseurs à Cheval. Troopers, Elite Company, 1810

The first six regiments of Chasseurs à Cheval were raised in 1779, six more being added in 1788. The strength of the arm had been increased to twenty-six regiments by 1801, and by thirty-one by 1811. These regiments made up the bulk of the French light cavalry.

Originally the Chasseurs à Cheval were dressed, hussar-style, in braided dolmans and mirliton caps, but in 1804–6 the 'surtout' jacket as illustrated was adopted. Black shakos were worn by the Chasseurs à Cheval at this time, though the Elite companies (the equivalent of the Grenadier companies in the infantry) in many cases continued to wear the bearskin 'colpack' or busby, with the red plume which signified their 'élite' status. The dark green surtout had cuffs, piping and sometimes the collar in the regimental facing colour (red for the 1st Regt.), and red epaulettes were worn by the élite companies; the other companies wore green shoulder-straps with piping of the facing colour. Officers were distinguished by silver lace, epaulettes and busby-cords, and by silver-laced pouches and belts. The equipment of the other ranks was white leather (tan for the 5th, 8th and 27th Regiments) with black pouches bearing the brass hunting-horn badge which symbolised the Chasseurs à Cheval; the élite companies had the more appropriate grenade as a badge. All ranks were armed with curved light cavalry sabres with brass hilts (gilt for officers), and the rank and file also carried carbines. The facings for the various regiments was as follows:

Regt.	Collar	Cuffs and Turnbacks
1	Scarlet	Scarlet
2	Green	Scarlet
3	Scarlet	Scarlet
4	Yellow	Yellow
5	Green	Yellow
6	Yellow	Yellow
7	Pink	Pink
8	Green	Pink
9	Pink	Pink
10	Crimson	Crimson
11	Green	Crimson
12	Crimson	Crimson
13	Orange	Orange
14	Green	Orange
15	Orange	Orange
16	Sky blue	Sky blue
17	Green	Sky blue
18	Sky blue	Sky blue
19	Light orange	Light orange
20	Green	Light orange
21	Light orange	Light orange
22	Dark orange	Dark orange
23	Green	Dark orange
24	Dark orange	Dark orange

Regt.	Collar	Cuffs and Turnbacks
25	Madder red	Madder red
26	Green	Madder red
27	Green	Madder red
28	Amarante red	Amarante red
29	Green	Amarante red
30	Amarante red	Amarante red
31	Chamois	Chamois

The 27th Regiment continued to wear the hussar-style dolman until 1814.

44. Westphalia: Garde du Corps. Officer, 1810

The Kingdom of Westphalia was created by Napoleon for his brother, Jerome Bonaparte, on 18 August 1807. In November 1807 King Jerome entered the Confederation of the Rhine, thus putting the Westphalian army at his brother's disposal. The uniforms of the Westphalian troops were closely copied from the French style.

The Garde du Corps was created in 1810 with a strength of one company to act as a Royal bodyguard at the Palace of Kassel, King Jerome's capital. The other ranks were drawn mainly from the former Polish Lancers who had escorted Jerome to his new Kingdom. The corps never saw active service.

The uniform of the Garde du Corps was French in style; the gilt helmet had a black bearskin crest and white plume, and bore a large front plate inscribed with the cipher of the King, 'J N' (Jerome Napoleon). The dark blue coatee had red facings, the collar being embroidered in gold with gold epaulettes (yellow for the rank and file), and on the right shoulder a gold aiguillette was worn. The steel cuirass had a red lining and 'cuffs' to protect the uniform, and bore a large gilt 'sunburst' plate on the front, which also carried the King's cipher. The white buckskin breeches were replaced by blue ones in winter. Equipment was white leather for the rank and file, and black leather with gold lace for officers. The guard of the officers' sword, which had a three-barred gilt hilt, also bore the 'J N' motif, as did the holster-caps of the dark blue shabraque.

The 'Gala' uniform of the Garde du Corps consisted of a white coat with dark blue collar, cuffs and lapels, with gold lace and gilt shoulderscales. This coat was worn with the helmet, breeches and equipment previously described.

45. Switzerland: Légion Sainte-Galloise. Artilleryman and Grenadier, 1810

Uniforms of the Swiss forces were modelled on the French style, and the troops of each canton had their own distinguishing features in their dress.

This plate illustrates the uniform of the 'Légion Sainte-Galloise', the militia of the small canton of St. Gall. The 'legion' system of incorporating two or more arms (e.g. infantry and artillery) in the same integral unit was used extensively throughout Europe during the Napoleonic period.

Both uniforms illustrated were predominantly French in style, the cut of the coat and breeches closely following the French pattern. A curious feature of this uniform was the drooping hair plume worn on both the grenadier's bearskin cap and the artilleryman's bicorn. The gaiters worn by the artillery were cut short, to resemble boots. The arms and equipment were also French in style; the artilleryman's cross-belt had a brass match-case affixed to the front.

46. Bavaria: Regimental surgeon; Saxony: Surgeon, Prinz Friedrich August Regiment of Infantry, 1810

The medical services of all the European nations were hopelessly inadequate to cope with the immense number of casualties caused by the Napoleonic Wars. Almost the whole of the medical services of the countries involved consisted of regimental surgeons, each battalion or regiment including one or more medical officers in their strength. There was little organisation for the treatment of the wounded beyond the insanitary field hospitals. Even in these hospitals conditions were appalling and techniques of surgery rudimentary in the extreme. France was one of the few nations to attempt a larger-scale organisation of medical service, with the 'flying ambulances' of Baron Larrey, who organised the 'Service de Santé'. Even this was totally inadequate to deal effectively with the casualties caused by the battles of the Napoleonic Wars.

The uniforms of regimental medical officers, though generally conforming in style with those of the regiment to which they were attached, lacked the epaulettes, lace and other features which were reserved for combatant officers. Surgeons' uniforms were of necessity as functional as the military fashions of the day would allow. The Bavarian medical officer (illustrated left) wore a dark blue coat and breeches with red facings and coat-tail lining, with plain silver lace on the collar and cuffs. The Saxon surgeon, of the Prinz Friedrich August Regiment of infantry, wore a pale grey coat with light green facings, with white turnbacks, and buff overalls with brass buttons. The bicorn hats were covered with oilskin in campaign dress. The surgeon's medical equipment was carried in a leather satchel slung over one shoulder. The Saxon officer carried a light-bladed sword with a brass hilt and black leather sword-knot, in a black scabbard with brass fittings, suspended from a white waistbelt.

47. France: Engineers of the Imperial Guard, 1810. Privates and Officer

On 1 July 1810 a fête was given at the Austrian Embassy in Paris. The event ended in disaster when the ballroom caught fire, the Russian Ambassador being injured and Princess Schwartzenburg burned to death. Napoleon himself directed the fire-fighting operations until 3 a.m., and concluded that the fire precautions at the Imperial Palaces were inadequate. He wrote: 'There shall be raised before 1 January 1811 a company of sapeurs-pompiers of the Imperial Guard under the Commandant of Engineers. This company will be assigned to serve the pumps at the Imperial palaces of Paris, Saint-Cloud, Versailles, Meudon, Rambouillet, Compiègne, Fontainbleau, etc. . . .' As a result of this order, the 'Sapeurs du Génie' of the Imperial Guard was formed on 16 July 1810.

The original strength consisted of one captain, two lieutenants, and 121 other ranks, equipped with a four-horse caisson and eight fire-pumps, each drawn by two horses and manned by six men. In 1813 the strength of the corps had risen to 250, and reached battalion strength by 1814, when it was disbanded. It was re-formed on 8 April 1815 during the 'Hundred Days' campaign. In time of war, the unit was attached to the Imperial Headquarters.

The uniform of the Engineers of the Imperial Guard was similar to that of the Engineers of the line, consisting of a dark blue uniform with black facings and red piping. The main distinguishing feature was the steel helmet with brass fittings (gilt for officers), with a large bearskin crest and red plume. On active service, the white gaiters of the rank and file were replaced by black ones.

Weapons and equipment were of the regulation infantry pattern.

The helmet was extensively copied by the various corps of 'Sapeurs-Pompiers', which were of a quasi-military nature, until the Second Empire. Paris had a battalion of Sapeurs-Pompiers in 1811, formed by the Fire Guards of the City, which became a regiment in 1865.

48. France: Vistula Legion, c. 1810. Voltigeur and Voltigeur bugler, 2nd Regiment; Private, 4th Regiment

The remnants of the Polish corps which had fought in Italy (see Plate 4) were formed in November 1807 into the 'Légion Polacco-Italienne', part of the army of Westphalia. In March 1808 it was transferred to the French army with the title of the Vistula Legion, with a strength of three regiments of infantry and one of lancers. In 1810, a fourth regiment of infantry and another of lancers were added; in June 1811, however, both regiments of lancers were detached to form the 7th and 8th Chevau-Légers of the French army, leaving only the four infantry regiments in the Vistula Legion. The Legion served with great distinction in the Peninsular War and in the Russian campaign of 1812, suffering severe losses; in June 1813 the four regiments were amalgamated to form the Vistula Regiment, which was finally disbanded in 1814.

The uniform of the infantry was based on the French pattern. Contemporary sources give conflicting information about the smaller details of the uniform. The dark blue jacket was faced differently for the four regiments: 1st Regt., blue collar and yellow cuffs; 2nd Regt., yellow collar and cuffs; 3rd Regt., yellow collar and blue cuffs; 4th Regt., blue collar and cuffs. However, one contemporary source shows the facings of the 4th Regiment crimson, as illustrated. Grenadier companies were distinguished by red shako plumes and epaulettes, and Voltigeurs by plumes, epaulettes and shako-cords in various combinations of the 'Voltigeur colours' of yellow, green and red. The shako bore a large brass plate of a 'sunburst' design, with the French cockade above. The lapels of the jacket are shown by contemporary authorities as either extending to the waist, or 'half-lapels' as illustrated on the central figure of the bugler, who carried a horn with cords of mixed red and white. Weapons and equipment were of the regulation French pattern.

49. Hesse–Darmstadt: Chevau-Légers. Trooper, 1810

The Landgrave of Hesse (later elevated to Grand Duke), Ludwig X, allied with Napoleon by joining the Confederation of the Rhine in January 1806. The Hessians were the last of his allies to abandon Napoleon in 1813.

The Hessian Chevau-Légers (light

horse) were raised on 6 April 1790, with a strength of three squadrons, and participated in numerous campaigns of the Napoleonic Wars, including the battles of Essling and Wagram; but the regiment's real glory came on 28 November 1812, at Studianka, when, protecting the retreating Grande Armée, the Chevau-Légers, together with the Baden Hussars, charged an overwhelming number of Russian cavalry. From the 'Charge of Death' only fifty men returned, and when the regiment arrived at Darmstadt its strength was only forty-two men and twenty-one horses. The survivors of this magnificent corps were almost annihilated in the campaign of 1813 at Juterbogk, where the Colonel, de Munchingen, was killed.

The uniform illustrated was that adopted in 1809, before which date long-tailed coats and small leather caps were worn. In 1809 the black leather helmet popular with the armies of numerous German states was adopted. The fittings were brass (silver for officers), and the badge worn under the front of the black woollen crest consisted of the crowned monogram of Ludwig X. The black and red plume issued from a cockade in the national colours of red and white. The coatee was dark green, with 'half-lapels' which exposed the bottom of the waistcoat. The red collar had a black patch on the front. Lace was silver for officers and white for other ranks, and officers wore silver epaulettes. The green overalls with black leather reinforcements worn

on active service were replaced by white breeches in full dress; officers wore green breeches and Hessian boots. The sword belt was white leather, though the pouch and carbine belts were black or buff. Officers' belts were covered with silver lace. Contemporary artists show several versions of the green shabraque, with black or white lace edging and sometimes bearing the crowned monogram of Ludwig X; officers' shabraques were laced with silver.

50. France: 2nd Chevau-Légers-Lanciers of the Imperial Guard. Officer and troopers, 1810

The 2nd Regiment of Chevau-Légers-Lanciers of the Imperial Guard was formed in September 1810 from the Royal Dutch Hussars and the Dutch Garde du Corps, with a strength of 748 men. The regiment was increased to 1,400 by 1812 for the Russian campaign, in which the regiment served with great distinction, and from which barely 200 returned. In January 1813 the regiment consisted of eight squadrons, each of 250 men. Two more squadrons were added from the Paris Municipal Guard; by this time only the first four squadrons were composed of Dutch, the remainder being French. The regiment was disbanded on the abdication of Napoleon in 1814, four squadrons being taken into the new Royal Guard. During the 'Hundred

Days' campaign these four squadrons were placed with the squadron of Polish Lancers in the combined regiment of Chevau-Légers-Lanciers of the Imperial Guard, which served at both Quatre Bras and Waterloo. The corps was finally disbanded on 20 September 1815.

The distinctive scarlet colour of the uniforms was taken from that of the Royal Dutch Hussars, and gave the regiment its nickname of 'the Red Lancers'. The style was taken from that of the 1st Chevau-Légers-Lanciers of the Guard, and was predominantly Polish, consisting of the czapka with 'sunburst' plate bearing a crowned 'N', the 'kurtka' (Polish-style jacket), and overalls. The whole uniform was scarlet, with dark blue facings and piping and yellow lace and aiguillettes (gold for officers). On campaign, the czapkas were covered with oilskin, and the white plumes removed, and the scarlet overalls were replaced by ones of a fawn colour. There was also a regiment 'tenue de route' (marching order) consisting of a sky-blue, double-breasted blouse with a red collar and brass buttons.

On active service, officers wore white leather belts and equipment like the men, but in full dress their pouch-belts and sword-belts were gold-laced, their rank being further indicated by a gold sash with blue lines. Officers wore gold epaulettes in all orders of dress, and their full-dress overalls had gold stripes down the outer seam. Greatcoats were dark blue for officers and sky blue with scarlet collars for other ranks. Until

1813 all ranks were armed with sabres and pistols, and the rank and file with lances; from that year, however, only the front rank carried lances, the rear ranks receiving carbines and bayonets instead. Shabraques were dark blue, with yellow lace edging and yellow crowned eagles in the rear corners; the saddles were covered with black sheepskin with a yellow 'wolf's tooth' edging. Officers' shabraques were of a similar design, but with gold lace, and saddle-covers of pantherskin.

51. Britain: 2nd Greek Light Infantry. Privates, 1813

The Greek Light Infantry was originally raised by Major Richard Church in the British possessions of the Ionian Islands, for local defence, in 1809. The colonelcy was given to Major-General Sir John Oswald, with Church as Major. Field officers (or 'Inspectors' as they were known in the corps) and Staff were British, the company officers being Greek chieftains from the mainland, and the rank and file were their tribesmen. A second regiment was raised in 1813, Church being appointed commanding officer with the rank of lieutenant-colonel. The 1st Regiment, having the Duke of York as nominal lieutenant-colonel, was granted the title 'Duke of York's Own', though this privilege was not extended to the 2nd Regiment. The corps served at the siege of St. Maura, and was disbanded in 1814.

The uniform of both regiments reflected the traditional Greek costume, and several versions are given by contemporary artists. The headdress was a close-fitting red cap with a brass plate, and a white turban for officers; a loose white shirt was worn underneath a red waistcoat, with a red jacket, and the traditional Greek 'skirt' or 'fustanella' worn over white breeches and red stockings, which according to some contemporary pictures were sometimes worn with green cross-garters (gold for officers). The jacket and waistcoat were trimmed and laced with the facing colour (yellow for the 1st Regiment, and green for the 2nd). The short ankle-boots were of brown leather. The officers' uniform was basically similar, with a profusion of gold lace, and a crimson sash over the right shoulder. One portrait of an officer of the 2nd Regiment, however, shows the most picturesque uniform of the entire period; the jacket was scarlet gold lace and embroidery, worn over a classical bronze cuirass; the headdress was a black leather, dragoon-style helmet with brass fittings, including a large brass lion's head on the front, and fitted with a long black horsehair tail; and the legs were covered by red greaves heavily decorated with gold and terminating at the knees with embossed brass lions' heads.

Equipment was in black leather for the rank and file, who were armed with a carbine and brass-hilted sword-bayonet, a pistol, and, according to one contemporary source, a short, wide-bladed knife. Powder-horns with brass fittings were carried from green 'flask-cords' on the cross-belt. Officers carried pistols and sabres of various elaborate designs, including one which had a crimson scabbard and gilt fittings.

52. Saxony: Private, Jäger Corps, 1813; Private, Light Infantry, 1810

A regiment of light infantry was added to the Saxon army in 1809, and in 1810 the rifle companies of the various infantry regiments were combined to form the 1st and 2nd Regiments of Jägers.

The uniforms of both corps were similar in design and colouring. The jackets were dark green, those of the light infantry being double-breasted. Both wore black cuffs, and the Jägers black collars also; the light infantry had green collars with black collar-patches. Shoulder-straps were black, and piping red, for both; the turnbacks of the light infantry were of a lighter shade of green. Both corps wore brass buttons. The light infantry wore grey breeches and black half-gaiters; the Jägers also wore grey breeches, but distinguished by red lace and 'darts' on the thighs. In 1813 they adopted grey overalls with a black stripe, piped red, down the outer seams.

Shakos were black, with white cockades worn underneath large green plumes, for both Jägers and light infantry, the former having green cords and the latter white. The Jäger shakos bore shield-shaped brass plates, while the light infantry had brass hunting-horn badges. In campaign dress, the shakos were covered with oilskin, and the large plumes were replaced by pom-poms or short 'tufts'. The light infantry bore their hunting-horn badges on the oilskin cover.

Equipment for both corps was of black leather, the canteens being borne on brown straps. Pouches of both corps bore the hunting-horn badge, and knapsacks were of brown hide. Both units carried brass-hilted short swords.

53. France: 1st (Polish) Chevau-Légers-Lanciers of the Imperial Guard, 1811. Trooper and Officer

When Napoleon entered Warsaw he was escorted by a guard of honour composed of Polish noblemen and was so impressed by their bearing that he created, on 2 March 1807, a regiment of four squadrons, totalling 968 men, of 'Chevau-Légers Polonais' for his Imperial Guard. In 1809 they were issued with lances, and became the 1st Chevau-Légers-Lanciers of the Guard, the famed Polish Lancers. In 1812 another squadron was added, the regiment having a strength of 1,500. They served in many campaigns, particularly distinguishing themselves at Wagram, though their most famous exploit was in Spain, when, on 30 November 1808, a single squadron of

150 men charged the hitherto impregnable position of Somosierra. In the seven minutes charge, they broke the Spanish position, overrunning and capturing four batteries of artillery. Eighty-three of the Poles became casualties, including all seven officers. When Napoleon was exiled to Elba, 120 faithful Polish Lancers accompanied him, and, serving in the combined regiment of Guard Lancers during the 'Hundred Days', saw action at Ligny. The corps was disbanded on 1 October 1815.

The uniform was typically Polish in style, like that of the 2nd Guard Lancers (see Plate 49). The czapka and the facings and piping of the 'kurtka' were in the distinctive crimson colour of the regiment. The cockade of the czapka bore a silver Polish cross in the centre. Until 1809, the rank and file wore a white epaulette on the left shoulder and a white aiguillette on the right; after that date, the positions were reversed. Epaulettes and lace were silver for officers. In service dress, the lapels were worn crossed over in such a manner that the crimson facing colour showed only as a thin piping at the edge, the remainder being blue. Blue trousers with two crimson stripes were worn in full dress, being replaced by blue overalls with a single crimson stripe and black leather reinforcements on campaign. In full dress, officers wore crimson trousers with silver lace.

Equipment was of white leather for the rank and file, officers' belts being laced silver. In full dress, officers wore the sash as illustrated; in other orders of dress, this was replaced by a silver-laced waist-belt, fastened by a silver plate bearing a gilt eagle. Senior officers had a special parade kurtka of white with crimson facings and silver lace. Greatcoats were white with crimson collars for the rank and file, and officers wore blue cloaks with crimson collars. Officers' shabraques were like those of the other ranks (as illustrated), but with silver lace and a pantherskin saddle-cover. When on parade, officers did not carry the valise, but at other times this was crimson with silver lace.

Originally all the rank and file were equipped with the lance, but eventually only the front rank carried them, in addition to a sabre and pistols. The rear ranks carried carbines and bayonets to replace the lance. Lance-pennons were of the distinctive crimson and white, though on campaign they were carried furled round the lance, secured by a black cover.

A third regiment of Chevau-Légers-Lanciers of the Imperial Guard was created on 5 July 1812; their uniform was like that of the 1st Regiment, but with yellow lace (gold for officers). They were practically annihilated in the Russian campaign, and the few survivors were merged with the 1st Regiment.

54. Spain: 7th Lancers of La Mancha. Trooper, c. 1811

Napoleon appointed his elder brother Joseph as King of Spain in May 1808, which aroused the hostility of a large proportion of the Spanish population, the resulting war driving the French out of the Iberian Peninsula and largely contributing to the downfall of Napoleon. Joseph, in a futile attempt to prop up his precarious régime, tried to raise a native Spanish army to assist the French forces. The attempt was unsuccessful, the Spaniards he did enlist being regarded as traitors by the remainder of the population. One Spanish infantry corps, the Regiment Joseph Napoleon, was a part of the Grande Armée in the Russian campaign.

One of Joseph's 'native army' regiments was the 7th Lancers, as illustrated. The black leather helmet with woollen crest was like that worn by the Spanish Chasseurs à Cheval from 1805. The short-tailed jacket was brown, with red facings and yellow lace (gold for officers); the yellow collar had a red collar-patch. The padded 'shoulder-rolls' were laced with yellow. Officers wore a gold epaulette on the left shoulder and a gold aiguillette on the right. Overalls were brown, with a red stripe on the outer seam (gold for officers).

Equipment was of white leather for the rank and file, and gold-laced red leather for officers. The green shabraques of the other ranks were laced with yellow, and had a scalloped edge with red piping; officers' shabraques were made of leopardskin, with a green scalloped edge and gold piping. All ranks were armed with sabre and pistols, and the rank and file also carried lances.

55. France: The Valaison Battalion, c. 1810. Corporal of Grenadiers and Fusilier

By an agreement of 8 October 1805, the Valais Canton of Switzerland undertook to supply a battalion of infantry to the French army, with a strength of 661 men. Formed at Genes, the Valaison Battalion served in the Peninsular War, behaving with conspicuous heroism at the Siege of Gerona, where they suffered severe losses. In 1810, Valais was annexed by France as the Department of Simplon, and the Valaison Battalion disbanded on 27 September 1811, the personnel being transferred to the 11th Light Infantry.

As with numerous Swiss corps in French service, the Valaison Battalion wore uniforms of the same cut as the French infantry, but of the distinctive scarlet colour. The facing colour of the Battalion was white. Grenadiers were distinguished by a yellow grenade badge on the collar, and by white epaulettes; the epaulettes of the Voltigeurs had red straps, green fringes and yellow 'crescents'; Fusiliers had red shoulder-straps with white piping. Officers had gold lace and epaulettes. Buttons were gilt for officers and brass for other ranks, inscribed 'Battalion Valaison' and 'Empire Français'.

Shakos were of the French pattern, Grenadiers having red plumes and cords, Voltigeurs yellow over green plumes, and Fusiliers green pompoms and white cords. Shako-plates were of the regulation 'Eagle' design. Officers'

shakos had gold cords and plumes like those of the rank and file, except for the senior officers, who like their counterparts in the French army were distinguished by white plumes. Breeches, gaiters and equipment were all of the regulation French pattern; greatcoats were dark blue. The undress forage cap or 'bonnet de police' (as illustrated) was an item of dress common to all arms of the French service, being worn in camp, on fatigue duties, and frequently on campaign. Those of the Valaison Battalion were scarlet with white piping.

56/57. France: Neuchâtel Battalion. Gunner, Artillery; Gunner, Artillery; Driver, Artillery Train; Driver, Artillery Train; Private, Engineers; Officer, Artillery, c. 1812

In 1806 the principality of Neuchâtel was annexed by France, Marshal Berthier being created Prince of Neuchâtel on 30 March. On 11 May 1807 a battalion of infantry was raised in Neuchâtel, under nominal command of the Prince. On 27 August 1808 a company of artillery was attached to the battalion, including detachments of Engineers and Artillery Train (drivers). The Battalion served in the Austrian campaign of 1809, and was then sent to Spain, where its main duty was to keep the French lines of communication open by protecting supply trains from the guerrillas. In this harassing task, they were employed against the savage Don Julian Sanchez, neither side showing mercy. In 1812, the Battalion was withdrawn from Spain to form part of the Grande Armée in the campaign in Russia. The corps was gradually worn down by enemy action, disease and cold, the artillery being lost at Krasnoie. The corps had embarked on the campaign with a strength of 1,027; only thirteen officers and seven men returned to the Regimental depot at Besançon. The Battalion was re-formed, and saw action at Lützen, Bautzen, Dresden, Leipzig and Hanau, and suffered so heavily that only a company was left. These remnants defended the depot at Besançon until 17 April 1814, even though Napoleon had abdicated on 6 April. What remained of the Battalion was disbanded on 1 June 1814.

The uniforms of the Neuchâtel Battalion were like those of the French infantry in style, though of the distinctive yellow colour, with red facings, which gave the Battalion its nickname of 'the canaries'. The artillery, engineers and artillery train were dressed in the same style, though in dark blue, with different coloured facings; yellow collar, cuffs and piping for the artillery; blue collar and cuffs, yellow lapels, and red piping for the engineers; and yellow collar and grey cuffs for the artillery train. Blue breeches were worn by all these except the drivers of the artillery train, who wore buckskin breeches and riding-boots; the breeches of the artillery had a yellow stripe down the outer seam. Arms and equipment were of the regulation French pattern, the pouches of the artillery bearing brass badges in the shape of crossed cannons.

58. France: 30th Chasseurs à Cheval, 1811. Officers

On 3 February 1811 the 30th Chasseurs à Cheval of the French army were raised in Hamburg, mainly from German recruits. The original intention was to form the corps as 'Chasseurs-lanciers', wearing Polish-style lancer uniforms in the traditional green colouring of the Chasseurs à Cheval. However, a shortage of green cloth meant that only a few received the correct uniforms. Instead, there was an abundance of red cloth in Hamburg, and this was made up into kurtkas for the remainder of the corps. The facings and piping of both the green and red uniforms were chamois, and officers' lace was silver. There was also a stable dress consisting of a pale grey, tailless jacket, with chamois collar. The czapkas were red, having a black plume with green top and white cords (silver for officers) in full dress. Plain black bicorns with white plumes were much favoured by the officers. Officers wore baggy green pantaloons 'à la mameluke', with a chamois stripe piped silver down the outer seam; other ranks wore red overalls with black leather reinforcements and a black stripe. The shabraques were green with chamois lace edging and silver piping for officers, and red with black lace for other ranks.

On 18 June 1811 the regiment was designated the 9th Chevau-Légers-Lanciers, and should have changed their uniforms accordingly to the regulation blue with chamois facings and blue piping, of the same style as previously worn. However, in 1812 the predominant colour was still red, for they were nicknamed the 'red lancers of Hamburg' during the Russian campaign, in which they served with distinction. It is possible that in late 1812 the czapkas had been changed to blue, and later the kurtkas also, but the red trousers were in use until 1813, when the regiment was re-formed and re-equipped in the regulation blue. Shabraques were blue with chamois lace and silver piping for officers, and white sheepskin with chamois 'wolf's tooth' edging for the other ranks; senior officers had silver lace edging to the shabraques, and pantherskin saddle-covers. The corps was disbanded in 1814.

Equipment was in white leather for the rank and file, and predominantly black leather for officers, though they also wore white on occasion. Officers' belts were laced with silver, and had gilt fittings. The lances carried by the rank and file had chamois pennons.

59. Poland: General Officers, c. 1796

Polish national costume exerted a considerable influence over military fashion during the Napoleonic period. Austria had experimented with Polish uhlans (lancers) in 1781, who wore the traditional Polish cloth cap with a padded, squared-off crown and a fur band round the base. This early 'Konfederatka' cap became larger and, when a peak was added, began to develop into the famous 'czapka'.

In 1797 General Dombrowski's Polish troops in the Army of Italy introduced Polish styles into the French army. The first Polish corps in the French army, the 1st Chevau-Légers Polonais of the Imperial Guard, formed in 1807, brought the first major change in uniform style into the French army since the Revolution: the czapka, now fully developed into the familiar square-topped version, the short-tailed jacket with 'plastron' lapels, the 'kurtka'; and the loose, 'overall' trousers. The traditional Polish weapon, the lance, was adopted in 1809, and thereafter the lancer regiments were all clothed in Polish-style costume, including the czapka in many cases. In 1812, the French infantry replaced the long-tailed 'habit-veste' coat with a short-tailed jacket with closed lapels, the 'spencer', which owed much to the kurtka in design.

Polish costume was also adopted by other European nations, principally being used for regiments of lancers; Austria, Russia and Prussia all had Polish-style regiments during the Napoleonic Wars. When Britain adopted the lance after Waterloo, the czapka and Polish jacket made their appearance in the British army for the first time.

The czapka, gradually becoming smaller as the nineteenth century progressed, became the standard lancer headdress throughout Europe, and remained so until the disappearance of full dress after the First World War.

Elements of the traditional Polish styles can be seen in Plate 59; the czapka and its predecessor, the short kurtka with 'plastron' lapels, and the overall trousers.

60. Saxony: Chevau-Légers, 1812. Officers, Polenz Regiment and Prinz Clemens Regiment

Saxony supplied 20,000 men to the Grande Armée which invaded Russia in 1812, including the four regiments of Chevau-Légers. These regiments, each with a strength of 670 men in four squadrons, were uniformed in the French style, and all wore the distinctive scarlet jacket, with different facing colours for each regiment: Regiment Prinz Clemens, light green; Regiment Polenz, blue; Regiment Prince Albert, dark green; Regiment Prince John, black. The facing colour was borne on the collar, cuffs, lapels and turnbacks.

The shako was in the French pattern, bearing a plate inscribed with the royal cipher, with a white plume and cords for the rank and file, and a white plume with black base and gold cords for officers. Officers were further distinguished by gold epaulettes. In full dress, white breeches and black riding-boots were worn, though on campaign these were replaced by grey overalls with a red stripe down the outer seam. These overalls had brown leather reinforcements on the inside, the edges of which were cut in a 'wolf's tooth' design, like that which edged the shabraques. The red shabraques were edged in the facing colour, those of the officers being piped with gold in addition. Portemanteaux were red with lace of the facing colour. Greatcoats were grey, with collars of the facing colour.

Equipment was white leather for the rank and file, and black leather with gold lace for the officers. All ranks were armed with the sabre, and the troopers with carbines. Regiment Prinz Clemens also carried lances; these bore pennons of green over red.

The Saxon Chevau-Légers saw much action in the Russian campaign, the Regiments Prinz Clemens and Polenz forming part of the 7th Corps, the Regiment Prince John the 9th Corps, and the Regiment Prince Albert the 3rd Cavalry Corps. All suffered heavy casualties; Regiment Prince Albert, for example, had scarcely 100 men alive after Borodino, of whom only fourteen officers and twelve men returned home.

61. Britain: 10th Prince of Wales' Own Royal Hussars. Trooper, 1812

The 10th Light Dragoons, raised in 1715, had adopted a hussar-style uniform by 1803, by the addition of fur caps (busbies), pelisses and barrelled sashes to their normal light dragoon uniform. In 1806 they became the first British regiment to be officially designated as Hussars, the title changing from 'Light Dragoons' to 'Prince of Wales' Own Hussars'; in 1811, the title changed again to the 'Prince of Wales' Own Royal Light Dragoons (Hussars)'.

The regiment served in the opening campaign of the Peninsular War, seeing action at Sahagun, Mayorga and Benavente in 1808; in the last action the 10th won great distinction, Private Levi Grisdall capturing the French General Lefevre-Desnouettes. Grisdall was promoted to sergeant by order of the Prince of Wales. Being evacuated at Corunna, the 10th returned to Spain in 1813, serving at Vittoria, where Captain Wyndham's squadron captured Joseph Bonaparte's carriage, Joseph himself only narrowly avoiding capture, and at Toulouse. In 1815, the regiment served at Waterloo.

Until February 1811, the blue hussar-style uniform had yellow facings and silver lace. The change of title necessitated a change to the scarlet facings of a 'royal' regiment; lace became gold in 1814. In 1814, blue facings were adopted. The lace of the rank and file was white, changing to yellow; the lace on the pelisse was of a distinctive pattern, the loops of braid being surrounded by a broad band of lace, known as 'the frame'. The lacing on the cuffs was, according to regimental tradition, an allusion to the Prince of Wales' feathers, the crest of their Colonel. The fur busbies had

red cloth bags and yellow cords (gold for officers), and white over red plumes. The officers' busbies were of the unusual pale grey colour, as was the fur on the pelisses of all ranks, though by about 1814 the fur of the rank and file had changed to black. In March 1813 scarlet shakos with yellow lace edging replaced the busbies; it is possible that prior to this date, the regiment had worn black shakos. The white breeches worn in full dress were replaced on active service by grey overalls with red stripes for the other ranks, and bright blue overalls with a gold stripe for officers. Shabraques were red with white lace (silver for officers) until about 1814, when they became blue with yellow lace (gold for officers); officers' shabraques had leopardskin saddle-covers, and their harness bore the unusual decoration of cowrie-shells. On active service, the shabraques of the rank and file were white sheepskin.

Equipment was of the regulation pattern, of white leather for the rank and file, and belts were gold-laced for officers. Sabretaches were red with gold and yellow lace in full dress, and covered with brown leather on campaign. The regiment was armed with the 1796 pattern light cavalry sabre, the rank and file also carrying carbines.

62. France: Corsican Regiment, c. 1812. Officer, Carabinier and Voltigeur

The Corsican Regiment was organised and uniformed as a corps of light infantry, the regimental distinction being the black facings and piping.

The French light infantry regiments were organised in the same manner as the line infantry; the 'centre' companies were known as 'Chasseurs', the élite companies (the equivalent of Grenadiers in the line) as 'Carabiniers', and the sharpshooters as 'Voltigeurs', as in the line. The uniform was of the normal infantry style, a dark blue 'habit-veste' coat, or 'spencer' after 1812. Lapels, cuffs and turnbacks were also dark blue, and the cuff-flaps red; the only distinguishing features of the various companies were the collar, epaulettes and the badges on the turn-backs (white hunting horns for chasseurs, red grenades for carabiniers and yellow or white hunting horns for voltigeurs). For chasseurs, the collar was red, piped white, and the green epaulettes had red 'crescents'. For voltigeurs, the collar was yellow, often piped red, and epaulettes in various combinations of yellow, red and green. For carabiniers, the collar was red with white piping, and epaulettes were red also. Waistcoats and breeches were dark blue. Gaiters were either black, like those of the line infantry, or 'half-gaiters' cut to resemble Hessian boots, with a trim and tassel in the appropriate colour – green for chasseurs, yellow for voltigeurs and red for carabiniers. Officers' distinctions were like those of the line infantry, though with silver lace and epaulettes in place of gold.

Shakos were of the same pattern as those of the line regiments; chasseurs had white cords and green plumes; voltigeurs green or yellow cords and plumes of green or yellow with red tops or bases; and carabiniers had red plumes and red or white cords. Frequently, carabiniers wore fur caps like line grenadiers, and on occasion voltigeurs are depicted in contemporary pictures wearing fur 'colpacks' or busbies, with yellow bags.

Equipment was like that of the line infantry; greatcoats were grey, brown or blue-grey. Short sabres were carried by carabiniers, voltigeurs and sometimes by chasseurs; they were distinguished by the colour of the tassel, red for carabiniers, green and red for chasseurs, and green, yellow and red for voltigeurs.

The above remarks are generalisations only; there were numerous variations and regimental distinctions in use throughout the period.

63. France: Lithuanian Tartars, c. 1812. Trooper

A squadron of light cavalry was formed by one Mustapha Achmatowicz from the Tartars of Lithuania on 24 August 1812. The unit was attached as scouts to General Konopka's ill-fated 3rd Chevau-Légers-Lanciers of the Imperial Guard, which was destroyed in the Russian campaign. The Tartars were reduced to company strength by the end of the campaign, and were attached on 9 December 1813 to the newly formed 3rd Eclaireurs (scout-lancers) of the Imperial Guard, with whom they served until Napoleon's abdication in 1814, the survivors returning home to Lithuania.

When originally raised, the oriental-style uniform varied greatly, according to contemporary pictures. The astrakhan-covered shako had a green bag, a yellow cloth turban, and brass badges in the form of stars and crescents. A loose green jacket was worn underneath a red waistcoat with yellow lace; the trousers were either green with red stripes, red with yellow stripes, or blue with yellow stripes. Shabraques were either red with yellow lace, or green with red lace. A different uniform was introduced in 1813, though it is probable that both styles were worn simultaneously. The 1813 pattern consisted of a black fur colpack with a green bag, white cords and a red plume, a crimson jacket, a yellow waistcoat with black braid, and blue trousers. The shabraques became plain blue, devoid of ornamentation, the saddles being covered with black sheepskin. The saddles were Eastern-style, sometimes with large 'open box' stirrups. Officers' uniforms were like those of the other ranks, but with a profusion of gold lace, and white plumes on the shakos.

The pouch-belt was white leather for the rank and file, and black with gold lace for officers; the pouch was black, and bore the Imperial eagle in brass (gilt for officers). Round the waist was worn either a white leather waist-belt with brass plate, or a yellow sash.

Sabres were mameluke-style, and all ranks carried a curved dagger thrust behind the sash or waist-belt. The rank and file carried lances, which had pennons of red over green or red over white.

64. France: Grenadiers of the Imperial Guard. Grenadier and Sergeant-Major, c. 1812

Originally formed as part of the Consular Guard, the Grenadiers of the Imperial Guard became the symbol of the Empire itself; they accompanied the Emperor on every campaign, being kept as an élite veteran reserve. The Grenadiers were vanquished only once, at Waterloo, when they were assailed by overwhelming numbers, fired upon at point-blank range by batteries of artillery, and overrun. The 1st Regiment of Grenadiers was formed on 2 December 1799, and the 2nd Regiment on 15 April 1806. The two were amalgamated in 1809. In September 1810 the Royal Dutch Guard became the 2nd (Dutch) Grenadiers, but on 18 May 1811 the old 2nd Regiment was re-formed, the Dutch Grenadiers becoming the 3rd Regiment. The Dutch Regiment was disbanded in February 1813, having been almost totally destroyed in the Russian campaign. During the 'Hundred Days', two more regiments were formed, the 3rd and 4th Grenadiers. All four fought at Waterloo, and were disbanded in September 1815.

The Grenadiers were uniformed in

the traditional blue 'habit-veste' coat, with white lapels and red cuffs and turnbacks. The epaulettes were red for Grenadiers, mixed red and gold for senior N.C.O.s, and gold for officers. The turnbacks bore the grenade badge in orange (gold for officers). The rank chevrons were orange for corporals, and gold with red edging for sergeants and senior N.C.O.s. White waistcoats showed under the open lapels, and white breeches were worn with white gaiters for parade and summer dress, and black gaiters for campaign and winter. Frequently, overall trousers were worn on campaign, of blue, white, grey or even brown. When not in full dress, officers often wore plain blue 'surtouts', with blue waistcoats, blue breeches and knee-boots.

The headdress was the distinctive black bearskin grenadier cap, with a copper plate (gilt for officers) on the front, bearing the Imperial eagle and grenades. The red cloth patch at the rear of the cap bore a white cross until 1808, and a white grenade thereafter (gold for officers and senior N.C.O.s). When the cap was not worn, for example on the march, it was carried on the knapsack in a blue and white striped cover, the plume being carried in a leather cylinder tied to the sword-scabbard. When the bearskin was not in use, black bicorns with orange lace and red pompoms were worn. The tricolor cockade was worn on both headdresses. The Dutch Regiment wore uniforms of a similar design, though of white with crimson facings.

Equipment was of white leather, of the regulation design. The knapsack was made of cowskin, and the black leather pouch bore a copper eagle and a copper grenade at each corner; on campaign the pouch had a white cloth cover with the eagle and grenades painted on in black. Greatcoats were blue; after 1812 some had red piping. All ranks carried swords, those of the rank and file being short, with brass hilts. The muskets carried by the Grenadiers were of a pattern made especially for them, with all the fittings other than the lockplate in brass.

65. Duchy of Warsaw: The Krakus. Officers, c. 1812

At the end of the Russian campaign, Prince Poniatowski began to re-organise the army of the Duchy of Warsaw, to reinforce the shattered Grande Armée. One of his new regiments was 'The Krakus', a corps of cavalry raised by a decree of 19 December 1812, and effective by April 1813. The corps, comprising four squadrons, was raised from the region of Cracow, and was similar to the Russian Cossacks; light cavalry, mounted on small, sturdy horses, capable of travelling large distances while scouting and skirmishing; they were, in fact, nicknamed the 'French Cossacks'. The regiment served throughout the campaigns of 1813 and 1814, with particular distinction in the defence of Paris.

Contemporary sources show two distinct types of uniform. In one style, illustrated right, the headdress was a round cap, of crimson pleated cloth with a white top, and white piping on each pleat; the base was edged in astrakhan, and there was a short white plume on the left. The coat was knee-length, of dark blue with crimson collar and cuffs, and, in place of a cartridge-pouch, two crimson pockets on the breast. Officers had silver lace and epaulettes to distinguish their rank. Trousers were blue, with crimson stripes and sometimes leather reinforcements. Officers wore black waistbelts, and the other ranks crimson sashes. Another version of the uniform (illustrated left), possibly worn later than the first version, had a small, crimson, czapka-style headdress, with a black astrakhan band; the coat had a crimson collar and astrakhan cuffs, and a crimson lining. The cartridge-pockets on the coat were replaced in this version of the uniform by black pouches, worn on a white cross-belt. Cloaks were grey, with hoods and sleeves, and were braided and edged with crimson.

Shabraques were dark blue with crimson lace for the rank and file, and silver lace with crimson piping for the officers, whose saddles were covered with black astrakhan. All ranks carried sabres and pistols, and the other ranks were also armed with the lance. Some of the lances had horse-tails fixed to the head, thus enabling messages to be passed at a great distance, by signalling with the lance, in the manner formerly used by the Turks.

66. France: The Isembourg Regiment, c. 1811. Carabiniers and Voltigeur Officer

The Isembourg Regiment was created on 1 November 1805, the commanding officer being the Prince of Isembourg. Recruiting was slow, and the regiment was eventually formed from foreigners, including many Austrian prisoners of war. Not unnaturally, with poor officers and other ranks of doubtful loyalty, the Regiment soon became infamous for bad discipline and numerous desertions. The Prince of Isembourg quickly relinquished command, and was replaced by Colonel O'Meara. The regiment served in Italy, including the attack on Capri, and in Spain, where its bad reputation became even worse. The mixture of poor troops of many nationalities (including sixty Spaniards in the 4th Battalion) gave the officers an impossible task in creating any sort of loyalty to the Emperor. In August 1811 this very mediocre corps was reorganised as the 2nd Foreign Regiment.

The Isembourg Regiment was uniformed and equipped in the manner of a light infantry corps. The uniform colour was a distinctive shade of light blue, with yellow collars and white piping. The chasseurs were distinguished by light blue shoulder-straps with white piping, the voltigeurs by green epaulettes with yellow 'crescents', and the carabiniers by red epaulettes. Shakos were worn by all companies, having red plumes and cords for carabiniers, green cords and green plumes with yellow tops for voltigeurs, and white cords for carabiniers. The carabiniers also wore bearskin caps with red plumes and white cords. Gaiters were knee-length, sometimes cut in the shape of Hessian boots. Equipment was of the regulation French pattern; the sabre-knots were red for carabiniers and green for voltigeurs. Officers were distinguished by silver lace and epaulettes, and wore black boots with silver edging. On occasion, the officers wore the bicorn in place of the shako; the plumes of the officers' headdress were like those of the other ranks, except for senior officers, who wore white plumes.

67. Cleve-Berg: Infantry. Officer and Grenadiers, c. 1812

In 1806 the Grand Duchy of Cleve-Berg was conferred upon Marshal Murat, who entered his new state into the Confederation of the Rhine on 12 July of that year. The Berg contingent to the Confederation forces consisted of 5,000 men, in four regiments of infantry, one of light cavalry, five companies of artillery and a detachment of engineers. Murat relin-quished the Duchy when he became King of Naples in 1808, and Napoleon gave the title to his nephew Louis, son of the King of Holland. The Berg army participated in the 1812 Russian campaign, the infantry forming part of the IX Corps. They proved themselves to be among the best troops in the Grande Armée; in spite of severe losses, they remained steady, and even at Kovno, when all had fallen to pieces, the remnants of the Berg infantry still stood to their colours.

The infantry were uniformed in the French style, the uniforms being based on the national colours of white and sky blue. Grenadiers were distinguished by red epaulettes, and fur grenadier caps which had red plumes and white cords. Fusilier companies wore the shako, with white cords and sky-blue pompom, and sky-blue shoulder-straps with white piping; voltigeurs had white shako-cords, green pompoms, and green epaulettes. Officers were distinguished by gold lace and epaulettes; in undress, they wore surtouts and breeches of pale grey, faced sky blue. Officers' bicorns were black, with gold lace and sky-blue pompoms. Arms and equipment were of the French pattern.

A unique feature of the Berg infantry was the dress of the Pioneers, who wore Grenadier uniform, with the addition of a white apron with red and sky-blue stripes round the edge, and lined with black fur. Like the Pioneers of the French army, they carried the customary axe.

68. Bavaria: Foot Artillery,
c. 1812. Officer and Private

Bavaria, as a member of the Conferation of the Rhine, provided 30,000 men to the Grande Armée for the invasion of Russia in 1812. The Bavarian Corps was virtually destroyed in the campaign, and Bavaria abandoned the Napoleonic alliance on 8 October 1813, thereafter fighting against her previous allies.

The Bavarian Foot Artillery was dressed in a similar style of uniform to the infantry, including the crested helmet or 'raupenhelm', which had brass fittings (gilt for officers), the national cockade of white and light blue, and the red plume which was characteristic of artillery units throughout Europe. The dark blue jacket had red collar, cuffs and turnbacks, and black lapels and cuff-flaps piped red. Epaulettes were gilt for officers and brass for other ranks, both having red-padded cloth linings. Breeches were blue, worn with black gaiters by the rank and file, and knee-boots by officers. Equipment was of the infantry pattern; on campaign, the grey greatcoat was worn rolled across the body. The Foot Artillery were armed like the infantry, the rank and file having brass-hilted short swords in addition to the musket. Prior to the introduction of the musket, they carried pistols suspended from a shoulder-belt.

The Artillery Train wore a uniform of a similar cut, in light grey with sky-blue facings, and light grey overalls with a sky-blue stripe down the outer seam. The Horse Artillery batteries wore a uniform similar to the Bavarian Chevaulegers.

69. Prussia: 10th (Colberg) Regiment, 1812. Grenadier and Musketeer

The Prussian army was completely reorganised in 1808, to contain twelve regiments of line infantry, of which the Colberg Regiment was numbered 10th. Prussian infantry regiments were composed of two battalions of musketeers, one of fusiliers (light infantry), and two companies of grenadiers. In December 1808 the grenadier companies were detached, to form separate Grenadier Battalions, those of the 10th Regiment combining with those of the 2nd to form the Pomeranian Grenadier Battalion; when 'on detachment', grenadiers wore the uniform of their parent unit. In June 1813, the Colberg Regiment was renumbered the 9th.

A new uniform was adopted in 1808, consisting of the dark blue 'Kollet' with red turnbacks, and facings which indicated the province from which the regiment originated: East Prussia, brick red; West Prussia, crimson; Pomerania, white; Brandenburg, scarlet; Silesia, lemon yellow; Magdeburg, light blue; Westphalia, rose; Rhine, crab red (the last three colours were added in 1814). These facing colours were borne on the collar and cuffs; the shoulder-straps indicated the seniority of the regiment: 1st Regiment, white;

2nd, scarlet; 3rd, yellow; 4th, light blue. Thus, with white facings and red shoulder-straps, the Colberg Regiment could be identified as the second Pomeranian corps. In 1813 the collar of the 'Kollet' was closed.

The shako, of the 1808 pattern, bore distinctive plates; the grenadiers wore a brass Prussian eagle, the musketeers the royal cipher, and the fusiliers a large black and white national cockade. All companies wore the black and white pompom, and in parade dress the grenadiers and fusiliers had a large black plume or 'busch'. In 1812 a different pattern of shako was introduced, with leather reinforcements on the sides. On campaign, the shako was covered with black waxed linen. Breeches were white for summer wear, and grey for winter, worn with black gaiters. Officers wore grey overalls with a red stripe down the outer seam on campaign; their uniform was otherwise basically similar to that of the other ranks, though the tails of the 'Kollet' were longer, their lace was silver, and they wore silver waist-sashes with black strands. Their shakos had gold lace, gilt chains and cock-feather plumes. N.C.O.s wore either gold or silver lace on their collars and cuffs, and the bottom of their plumes were white.

Equipment was of white leather for grenadiers and musketeers, and black for fusiliers, with calfskin knapsacks and black leather pouches. The pouches of grenadiers and musketeers had oval brass plates bearing the Prussian eagle. Greatcoats were grey, carried on top of the knapsack when not in use; on campaign, they were often carried rolled over the right shoulder. Short sabres were carried by grenadiers and musketeers, with sword-knots coloured to indicate the company. Fusiliers carried a distinctive straight-bladed sword on a shoulder-belt. Officers were armed with straight-bladed swords, though fusilier officers and some grenadiers carried sabres. The musket-slings were of a distinctive reddish-brown coloured leather.

70. Britain: 42nd Royal Highland Regiment (Black Watch), c. 1812. Officer and Private of Battalion companies

Raised in 1725, though tracing their descent from 1624, the 42nd Royal Highlanders (Black Watch) served with great distinction throughout the Revolutionary and Napoleonic Wars. At Geldermalsen in 1794, in the West Indies, at Minorca, at Alexandria in 1801, at Walcheren, and in the Peninsular War, at Corunna, Busaco, Fuentes de Onoro, Ciudad Rodrigo, Salamanca, Burgos, Vittoria, Nivelle, Nive, Orthes, Toulouse, and, finally, at Quatre Bras and Waterloo, the 42nd earned a reputation for bravery second to none in action, and one of gentleness and humanity towards civilians. There was no better corps in Europe than the 42nd, and the Regiment had very few equals.

The uniform was a mixture of

traditional Highland costume and regulation infantry uniform. The feather bonnet had a band of 'Highland dicing' of red, green and white, and bore the red hackle plume, adopted in 1795, a regimental distinction worn to the present day. The plumes were red for Battalion companies, red over white for the grenadiers, red over green for the light company, and red over yellow for drummers. Below the plume was a cockade, black for Battalion companies, red for the grenadiers, green-edged red for the light company, and red-edged black for drummers. The bonnets had a detachable leather peak. Unlike those of the other Highland regiments, the bonnets had 'flat' feathers, i.e. with no 'tails' hanging down the side of the bonnet.

The jacket was of the regulation infantry pattern, with dark blue facings. Battalion companies wore blue shoulder-straps with white worsted tufts, the flank companies wings with white fringes, and the officers epaulettes. Lace was gold for officers and white with a red stripe for other ranks, the lace loops on the breast and cuffs of the other ranks' jackets being in 'bastion' shape, evenly spaced. The kilts were made of '42nd' or 'Government' tartan; the Grenadiers wore the same set, but with the addition of a red overstripe. Pipers wore kilts of the Royal Stuart tartan. In full dress, officers wore a small 'fly' plaid of the regimental tartan. Sporrans were worn in full dress only. The hose were checked red and white, and supported by red garters; on active service, the rank and file wore grey half-gaiters. Officers wore grey or dark blue overalls on campaign, with two red stripes down the outer seam; for morning parades, they wore sky-blue overalls with a gold lace stripe, piped on either side with red. Officers were further distinguished by a crimson sash, worn over the left shoulder, and the gilt gorget, supported by ribbons of the facing colour. Sergeants' sashes were crimson with a blue central stripe, and their chevrons were of silver lace, a unique regimental distinction.

The equipment was of white leather of the regulation pattern, with a black pack and cartridge-pouch; the canteen was light blue, carried on a brown strap. Belt-plates were gilt with silver devices for officers, and brass for other ranks; both oval and rectangular versions existed. Officers, pipers and musicians carried the broadsword, officially (though incorrectly) known as a 'claymore'. This had a gilt or brass basket-hilt, lined with crimson or red cloth. Sergeants of the Battalion and Grenadier companies also carried the broadsword, in addition to their 'spontoon' or half-pike. Sergeants of the Light company and regimental pioneers were armed with curved, brass-hilted sabres; Field officers carried the normal infantry sword. In full dress, officers and pipers carried the ornamental dirk.

71. France: Aides de Camp, c. 1812. A.D.C. to a General, A.D.C. in campaign dress, A.D.C. to a General of Division

The Aides-de-Camp of the French army were officers ranking between Sub-Lieutenant and Colonel. Their duty was to transmit orders from the General Staff to units in the field, to carry messages between General Officers, and to reconnoitre enemy positions and to report on them to the Staff. For this purpose, every General Officer had a number of A.D.C.s attached to his personal staff. The Aides had to be excellent horsemen – one rode from Madrid to Bayonne in three days, avoiding guerrillas all the way. Because of the hazardous nature of their duties, the casualty rate was extremely high – it was not uncommon for a General to lose all his A.D.C.s in a major engagement.

Uniforms of the A.D.C.s were many and varied; there was a regulation uniform, authorised on 24 September 1803, but these regulations were often disregarded. Some Aides wore uniforms based on the dress of their own regiment; some, on secondment, simply added the A.D.C.s' brassard to their regimental uniform; others wore the basic regulation uniform with additions of their own design; and several of the Marshals designed unique uniforms for their A.D.C.s; the uniforms worn included every type and colour of shakos, colpacks, dolmans, pelisses and breeches.

The uniforms depicted in Plate 71 are those based on the 1803 regulations. The coatee was dark blue, with sky-blue facings and piping, with gold lace. On campaign, the single-breasted version (illustrated centre) was popular; the figure on the right wears a waistcoat and breeches of hussar style. On parade, white breeches were regulation, these being replaced by blue in other orders of dress. On campaign, overalls of various colours were adopted. Epaulettes were of various designs to distinguish rank, as in the rest of the army. The black bicorn was ornamented with gold lace, and black covers were often worn on campaign. The plume colour signified the rank of the General Officer to whom the A.D.C. was attached; red over white for the staff of a General, red over blue for a General of Division, and sky blue for a General of Brigade. The symbol of the A.D.C.s' position, the brassard worn on the left arm, was white for the A.D.C. of a General, scarlet for a General of Division, and sky blue for a General of Brigade. Greatcoats were dark blue, with collar and cuffs of sky blue.

Shabraques were dark blue with gold lace, with blue holster-caps for parade; bearskin holster-caps were used on campaign. Officially, belts were of black leather with gilt fittings, though numerous other types were worn. A.D.C.s were armed with a curved sabre, though personal preference was again more important than the official regulations in determining the pattern of sabre carried.

**72/73. Russia: Cuirassiers, 1812.
N.C.O., Czarina's Regiment;
Officer, Pskoff Regiment;
Officer, Military Order
Regiment; Trooper,
Pskoff Regiment; Officer,
Klein-Russland Regiment**

There were twelve regiments of cuirassiers in the Russian army, including the Chevaliers-Garde. The black leather helmet was introduced in 1803 with a woollen crest, but these were replaced in 1808 by horsehair crests. The fittings were brass (gilt for officers), the plate bearing the Imperial eagle; the Military Order Regiment bore the Order of St. George on their plates. The coatee was of the traditional white colour, with collar, cuffs and shoulder-straps of the facing colour, with yellow or white lace (gold or silver for officers):

Regt.	Facings	Lace
Chevaliers-Garde	red	yellow
Horse Guard	red	yellow
Life Guard	light blue	white
Czarina's	violet	white
Jekaterinoslaff	orange	white
Pskoff	dark red	yellow
Gluchow	blue	yellow
Astrachan	yellow	white
Military Order	black	yellow
Klein-Russland	dark green	yellow
Nowgorod	light red	white
Starodub	light blue	yellow

Until 1812, the collars were worn open to expose the black stock; in that year they became closed. Officers wore gilt epaulettes with a lining of the facing colour, and were further distinguished by waist-sashes of silver with orange strands.

As befitted their arm of service, all the regiments wore cuirasses. These were of black lacquered iron with gilt fittings for officers, for all except the Czarina's Regiment (which wore white metal cuirasses), and the Pskoff Regiment (which wore white metal for the rank and file, and gilt for officers). The cuirasses were lined with red cloth. In full dress, white breeches and black riding-boots were worn, but on campaign these were replaced by grey-brown overalls for the rank and file, and grey overalls with stripes of the facing colour for officers.

Shabraques were red, laced in white or yellow (silver or gold for officers) for all regiments except the Chevaliers-Garde (whose shabraques were edged with lace in a yellow–blue–yellow stripe), the Horse Guard (edged yellow–red–yellow), and the Life Guard, whose officers had shabraques edged with silver–white–silver. Shabraques and holster-caps were embroidered with the Imperial cipher. Equipment was of white leather.

The effectiveness of the cuirasses may be judged by an engagement at Shevardino in the 1812 campaign, when the 9th Chevau-Légers-Lanciers ('the red lancers of Hamburg') charged a formation of Russian cuirassiers in the gathering gloom of a September evening. The French did not realise that the Russians were wearing cuirasses until they met in what was virtually a head-on collision. Their lances, unable to penetrate the cuirasses of the Russians, the 9th were forced to fall back behind the French lines to reorganise.

74. Russia: Infantry, 1812.
Private, Mohilev Musketeers;
Private, in greatcoat

Czar Alexander was responsible for the major reorganisations of the Russian army which took place between 1801 and 1812. The Russian infantry consisted of Grenadier and Musketeer regiments. Musketeer regiments, as illustrated, were organised in three battalions, each battalion comprising three companies of musketeers and one of grenadiers. Prior to 1807, the army was grouped in 'Inspections' or administrative areas, each 'Inspection' having a different facing colour; in 1807, the infantry were reorganised in Divisions, and red facings were adopted by all regiments.

The shako illustrated is the uniquely Russian 'kiwer', probably designed by the Czar himself and authorised on 1 January 1812. Pompoms were coloured differently for each company; N.C.O.s' pompoms were quartered, the top and bottom in black and orange, and the left and right in white; officers' pompoms were silver with an orange centre bearing the Imperial cipher. The dark green jacket prior

to 1807 had collar and cuffs in the facing colour of the 'Inspection': Brest, lemon yellow; Crimea, buff; Finland, yellow; Lithuania, light green; Moscow, orange; Petersburg, red; Ukraine, rose; Caucasus, medium blue; Dniester, dark green (lilac before 1805); Kiev, raspberry red; Livonia, sky blue; Orenburg, brown; and Smolensk, grey. The individual regiments of each 'Inspection' were identified by the colour of the shoulder-straps. When the 'Divisional' system was adopted in 1807, the collar and cuffs became red for all regiments. The only distinction was in the shoulder-straps, which were red for the 1st Regiment of each Division, white for the 2nd, yellow for the 3rd, dark green with red piping for the 4th, and sky blue for the 5th. Each strap bore the number of the division in red (in yellow on red shoulder-straps). Thus, the figure on the left can be identified as the 3rd Regiment of the 5th Division, which in 1812 was the Mohilev Musketeers. This regiment was formed in 1806–7 as part of the Lithuanian 'Inspection', and accordingly had light green collar and cuffs, the regimental distinction being grey shoulder-straps. After the 1807 reorganisation, they ranked as the 2nd Regiment of the 5th Division, and wore white shoulder-straps accordingly; in 1812 they became the third regiment of the Division, and adopted the appropriate yellow shoulder-straps. In 1812 they formed part of the 1st Army of the West.

In summer, one-piece gaiter-trousers

were worn; in winter these were replaced by trousers and gaiters, or by overalls with black sheepskin sewn on to the lower leg; officers wore grey overalls. Equipment was of white leather, with knapsack and pouch of black leather; musketeers bore brass grenade badges on the pouch, and grenadiers had a similar badge, with three flames. Officers also carried small packs. The greatcoat was made of a rough grey-brown cloth, with collar and shoulder-straps like the jacket. The greatcoat was much favoured by the Russian infantry, as it resembled the loose-fitting peasant costume; they were often worn on campaign in place of the jackets, which were put into store. When not in use, the greatcoat was carried rolled over the left shoulder, as a protection against sword-cuts. The undress cap was green with regimental piping, those of the officers having black leather peaks.

75. Württemberg: Artillery, c. 1812. Officer, campaign dress; Gunner; Officer, Undress

In 1806 the artillery of the Württemberg army was a small unit, with only 466 of all ranks in its strength. By 1809 the strength had increased to three batteries, with a total of twenty-two guns, and in 1812, when the Württemberg contingent marched into Russia with the Grande Armée as part of the forces of the Confederation of the

Rhine, there were two batteries of Horse Artillery and two of Foot Artillery, each equipped with six guns. The Horse batteries were armed with twelve-pounder cannon, and the Foot batteries with seven-pounder howitzers. All the artillery was lost in the retreat. In early 1813, one battery of Horse and one of Foot Artillery were reconstituted; the Horse Artillery was a particularly fine corps, armed with six-pounder cannon and equipped even better than the French. In May 1813, twelve more guns joined the field army, but the strength was quickly reduced by the campaigns of that year. After Leipzig, Württemberg abandoned the French alliance and joined the Allies.

The Württemberg artillery was uniformed in the French style, though retained the distinctive 'raupenhelm' or crested helmet which was introduced in 1804. Until 1810, the black leather helmet bore an oval brass plate on the front, inscribed with the Arms of the state; after that date, the larger brass plate, as illustrated, was adopted, including grenade-shaped chinscale bosses. In 1813 French-style shakos with yellow cords replaced the 'raupenhelm'. In undress uniform, officers wore black bicorns.

The jacket was light blue, with black collar and cuffs; until 1810, black lapels had also been worn, but in that year the style was changed to one with light blue half-lapels with yellow piping, as illustrated. Shoulder-straps were black with yellow piping for the rank and file, and officers were distinguished by gold epaulettes. Breeches were light blue, worn with black gaiters by the rank and file; on campaign these were replaced by grey overalls with black leather reinforcements. Equipment was of the French pattern, of black leather for officers and white for other ranks. Batteries attached to the Württemberg Guard wore a similar uniform, but with loops of white lace on the collar, cuffs and lapels, and white cords when the shako was introduced. Horse Artillery also wore a similar uniform, with metal shoulder-scales in place of epaulettes and shoulder-straps.

76. France: 4th Swiss Infantry, 1812. Officers

Swiss troops had long been used in the French service, the Swiss Guard of the Ancien Régime dying at the Tuileries in 1792. In 1798 there were six Helvetian demi-brigades in the French army, and by a Treaty of 27 September 1803, Switzerland agreed to supply France with 16,000 men, organised in four regiments of infantry, each with a company of artillery. On 15 October 1806 the 4th Swiss Regiment was formed. From the time of the Swiss Guard of the French monarchy, the Swiss had been noted for their courage and devotion, and, when the Swiss regiments took part in the Russian campaign of 1812, they proved themselves to be among the finest in Europe. At the crossing of the Beresina, when the line had to be held

to save the Grande Armée, it was the Swiss who fought until their ammunition was expended, and then charged with the bayonet. They held the line, but in doing so lost 80 per cent of their strength. 'They were, right to the end of the retreat, invincible; they outdid nature, and they spread a radiance of heroism into this desert of snow.' In 1814, the Swiss regiments returned to their native land, but during the 'Hundred Days' campaign a regiment was formed from the loyal Swiss. Brave to the last, they were wiped out in the attack on the bridge at Wavre.

The Swiss regiments wore uniforms like those of the French infantry, but in the distinctive red colour, with different facings for the four regiments: 1st Regiment, yellow, piped sky blue; 2nd Regiment, royal blue, piped yellow; 3rd Regiment, black, piped white; 4th Regiment, sky blue, piped black. Officers wore gold lace and epaulettes (the 1st Regiment having silver until 1812); the Grenadiers originally wore red epaulettes, but these were replaced by white ones, which showed more distinctly against the uniform (the 2nd Regiment wore blue epaulettes for a time, before adopting the white). Some of the Voltigeur companies wore yellow or chamois collars and shoulder-straps. Equipment and weapons were like those of the French infantry. The illustration shows the 'spencer' type of coat with closed lapels, which replaced the longer-tailed coat with 'open' lapels in 1812.

77. Saxony: Garde du Corps.
Officer, c. 1812

In 1810 the Saxon army was re-organised; there were three regiments of heavy cavalry, the Garde du Corps, the Cuirassiers of the Guard, and the Zastrow Cuirassiers, of which the senior regiment was the Garde du Corps. Both the Garde du Corps and the Zastrow Regiment served in the Russian campaign of 1812, as part of Saxony's contribution to the forces of the Confederation of the Rhine. Both regiments were heavily engaged at Borodino, where both lost more than half their strength in the attack on the great redoubt. In the retreat from Moscow, both regiments were destroyed, only twenty officers and seven other ranks from both corps reaching safety. The standards of both were lost, as were the famous silver trumpets of the Garde du Corps. Almost annihilated, the Garde du Corps took no further part in the Napoleonic Wars.

The uniform of the Garde du Corps was cut on French lines. The helmet was similar in style to that of the French Chevau-Légers-Lanciers, of brass with a black crest and fur turban, and a white over black plume. The fur turban was surrounded by a wreath of brass oak leaves on the helmets of the officers. The pale yellow jacket with blue facings was ornamented down the front of the breast, and on the collars, cuffs and turnbacks of the rank and file with a distinctive yellow lace, which had interwoven vertical stripes of red

and blue. Officers' lace was gold, as were their epaulettes and aiguillette, worn on the right shoulder; other ranks wore brass shoulder-scales. Breeches were white, worn with riding-boots. Shabraques were blue, laced in gold for officers and with the yellow, red and blue lace for other ranks. Equipment was made of white leather for the rank and file, and blue leather with gold lace for officers. Originally, the regiment was mounted entirely on black horses, but of course on campaign such regimental distinctions could not always be continued.

78. Hanover: Feldjägerkorps von
Kielmannsegge, c. 1814.
Sharpshooter and rifleman

The Hanoverian army was reconstructed in 1813 after the end of the French occupation. The corps of jägers illustrated was formed in the spring of 1813 with a strength of two companies, commanded at first by Jagdjunker von Düring, and later by Colonel Graf von Kielmannsegge from whom the regiment took its name. A third company was formed, and the corps was equipped with two two-pounder cannon, served by riflemen, and a section of twelve mounted riflemen was added. In October 1813 a fourth company was formed, and the whole corps disbanded in September 1814, though two companies were re-formed in 1815.

Both figures illustrated are taken from contemporary sketches, and differ in slight details. It is probable that both single-breasted and double-breasted versions of the jacket were worn simultaneously; the rank of sharpshooter was distinguished by the cloth epaulette on the right shoulder, riflemen having plain shoulder-straps of the light green facing colour. Buttons and badges were made of either brass or white metal. The soft-topped cap was strengthened up the sides with strips of black leather, and bore the hunting-horn badge of the jäger arm. The grey overalls were worn with short gaiters. Officers were distinguished by gold-laced 'wings' and sword-knots, and by British-style light infantry sashes. Equipment was made of black leather, the sword-bayonet being carried on a shoulder-belt, which bore the 'GR' cipher of King George III of England, who was of course Elector of Hanover. Powder-flasks were carried on light green cords; the hide knapsacks had brown leather straps. The corps was armed with rifled muskets.

79. Prussia: Landwehr Infantry, c. 1814. N.C.O., East Prussia; Private, Elbe; Private, 1st Silesian Regiment

The Prussian Landwehr or Militia was raised in 1813, a call to arms which involved all men between the ages of eighteen and forty-five. The Prussian economy, overstretched already to pay for the regular army, could not support the requirements of the Landwehr, and for the first year of their existence their equipment was wretched in the extreme. By 1814 the worst deficiencies had been overcome and by the time of Waterloo, when a Landwehr unit enjoyed the privilege of being the first Prussian regiment on the field, the Landwehr was adequately clothed and armed. The majority were raised as infantry (as illustrated), though numerous cavalry units existed.

The clothing and equipment was authorised on 17 March 1813; each man was supposed to supply his own uniform, but many were too poor, and received their clothing from either the town or district in which their regiment was raised, or from various patriotic organisations. The coat was a 'litewka', a loose-fitting garment of indeterminate length, varying from mid-thigh to well below the knee, of dark blue, black, grey and even brown cloth, with the collar and sometimes the cuffs of the provincial facing colour: East Prussia, orange-red; West Prussia, black; Brandenburg, brick red; Pomerania, white; Silesia, yellow; Elbe, light blue; Westphalia, green; Rhine, madder red; the last three being added in 1814. However, shortage of materials often resulted in deviations from the regulations. Shoulder-straps were often coloured to indicate seniority, as in the regular army; 1st Regiment, white; 2nd, red; 3rd, yellow; 4th, light blue; though this practice was not always used. By 1815 it was normal to have the regimental number embroidered on the shoulder-strap. Both single- and double-breasted versions of the litewka were worn.

The headdress was a soft-topped cloth cap or 'schirmütze', sometimes without peak, of the same colour as the litewka. From 31 May 1814 the caps were piped with the facing colour. They bore the black and white national cockade, and the white metal or cloth 'Landwehr cross', which bore the inscription 'Mit Gott für König und Vaterland'; this was the distinctive badge of the Landwehr until the First World War. The caps had black leather peaks, though peakless versions were occasionally worn; sometimes black waterproof covers were used, and some Silesian units at least wore British 'stovepipe' shakos, with the Landwehr cross on the front.

Breeches or trousers were made of white, dark blue or grey cloth, worn with a variety of black, white or grey gaiters; boots were rare in the early months of the corps' existence, wooden clogs being worn by many, and it was not uncommon for Landwehr men to go barefoot. Equipment was made of black and occasionally white leather, in numerous styles, with various designs of knapsack; canteens, water-bottles or gourds were worn on cords, and, when greatcoats were issued, these were often carried rolled over the shoulder as an added protection against sword-cuts. Officers were authorised to wear uniforms like those of the regular army, with the schirmütze of the Landwehr; but on campaign many adopted the litewka. Volunteers who held the rank of 'grefreite' were distinguished by a thin white braid round the cuff; sergeants had black braid, though mixed black and white braid was a common distinction for all grades of N.C.O.

When first raised, the arms of the Landwehr consisted of captured muskets and eight-foot-long pikes with six-inch heads; originally, only the second and third ranks were armed with muskets, the first rank carrying pikes; but by July 1813 muskets were carried by all. A large axe with a long beech-wood haft was carried by many, worn on a shoulder-belt. N.C.O.s carried sabres in addition to their muskets, and officers were armed as in the regular army.

The three uniforms illustrated show some of the numerous variations of the regulation uniform; the East Prussian N.C.O. wears the litewka in grey, with black and white braid indicating his rank; the Elbe private wears overalls, and the private of the 1st Silesian Regiment wears clogs, and has a small, non-regulation plume in his schirmütze. Large quantities of captured French equipment were used, and to illustrate how far non-regulation uniforms were worn, one Silesian formation is recorded as wearing 'red English hussar uniforms with a conical English shako'.

80. Russia: Light Infantry, c. 1814. Private, Carabinier Company, 39th Jägers; Private, Jägers; Private, Carabiniers

In 1810 the Russian army contained 32 regiments of Jägers. Regiments numbered 33 to 46 were formed by the conversion of fourteen musketeer regiments in that year, and by 1812 numbers 47 to 50 had been raised. In 1813 seven more regiments were formed, bringing the total number to 57. In April 1814 six regiments, the 1st, 3rd, 8th, 14th, 26th and 29th, were designated 'Jäger-Grenadiers', and in August were renamed as the 1st to 6th Carabiniers, acting as light infantry of the Grenadier Divisions.

In 1812 the Jäger regiments adopted the 'kiwer' shako in common with the other Russian infantry; their jackets were dark green with dark green facings and red piping for all regiments, the only distinguishing feature being the shoulder-straps, which bore the number of the Division to which the regiment was attached, as in the case of the line infantry. In 1812 yellow shoulder-straps were worn by the regiments numbered 1 to 11, 13, 16 to 20, 23, 25, 27 to 31 and 49; all the other regiments wore sky-blue straps. From April 1814, the six regiments of Jäger-Grenadiers adopted yellow straps,

and those regiments which previously wore yellow adopted sky blue, and those which previously wore sky blue adopted green with red piping. In August 1814 the Carabiniers adopted red shoulder-straps; each ordinary Jäger regiment also contained a Carabinier platoon.

The Jägers wore grenade badges on their shakos, and their cartridge-boxes bore the regimental number in brass. The battalions of each regiment could be identified by the cockades on their shakos; the 1st Battalion of each regiment wore white cockades with green centres, the 2nd green with white centres, and the 3rd light blue with white centres. Carabiniers wore red cockades, and in full dress tall black plumes.

In summer, white gaiter-trousers were worn, though in winter these were replaced by dark green overalls with a red stripe down the outer seam, often worn with black gaiters. Officers wore grey overalls with a double black stripe. Arms and equipment were like those of the line infantry.

SOURCES OF INFORMATION FOR THE ILLUSTRATIONS

1. Rousselot; contemporary gouache by Barbier.
2. Zweguintzow Collection.
3. Landsmuseum, Zürich.
4. 'Zolnierz Polski'.
5. 'Abbildungen der stehenden Herre Europas' (Steinacker 1803).
6. Knötel; contemporary pictures and items of uniform.
7. Malibran.
8/9. Malibran.
10. Landsmuseum, Zürich.
11. Rousselot; Malibran; items of uniform and equipment; Musée de l'Armée, Paris.
12. Hourtoulle; Knötel.
13. Olmes, after contemporary lithograph; Knötel.
14. Contemporary print; dress regulations.
15. 'De Nederlandse Infanterie' (H. Ringoir).
16. Contemporary print, Musée de l'Armée, Paris; dress regulations.
17. Knötel.
18. Contemporary print by Holtzmann; contemporary painting by Opitz; items of uniform.
19. Malibran.
20. Knötel.
21. Contemporary illustrations, Army Museum, Copenhagen, and Danish State Archives.
22. Knötel.
23. Knötel.
24/25. Knötel.
26. Olmes.
27. Malibran.
28. Knötel.
29. 'Prussian Army' (Pietsch); contemporary prints.
30. Knötel; contemporary pictures.
31. Olmes; Knötel; contemporary illustrations.
32. Army Museum, Vienna; contemporary pictures and items of uniform.
33. Knötel; Frankfurt Collection.
34. Olmes, after original lithographs.
35. Hourtoulle; contemporary illustrations.
36. After Carl Vernet.
37. Knötel.
38. Knötel.
39. Army Museum, Vienna; contemporary illustrations and items of uniform.
40/41. Contemporary illustrations and items of uniform and equipment.

42. *Olmes, after original lithographs.*
43. *Malibran.*
44. *Contemporary print by Sauerweid.*
45. *Landsmuseum, Zürich.*
46. *Olmes, after original lithographs.*
47. *Malibran.*
48. *'Zolnierz Polski' (Gembarzewski); 'Wojsko Polski'.*
49. *Hourtoulle, after contemporary illustrations.*
50. *Malibran.*
51. *'Costume of the Army' (C. H. Smith 1815); 'Military Costume of Europe' (Goddard & Booth 1812).*
52. *Knötel; Olmes, after contemporary lithographs; 'Le Manuscrit d'Elberfeld'.*
53. *Knötel; contemporary illustrations, etc.*
54. *Knötel.*
55. *After Carl Vernet and contemporary sources.*
56/57. *Hourtoulle.*
58. *Hourtoulle.*
59. *'Zolnierz Polski'; Army Museum, Warsaw.*
60. *Hourtoulle.*
61. *Contemporary print, National Army Museum, London.*
62. *Contemporary illustrations, etc.*
63. *Hourtoulle.*
64. *Malibran; actual items of uniform.*
65. *Hourtoulle.*
66. *Hourtoulle.*
67. *Knötel.*
68. *Knötel.*
69. *Knötel.*
70. *Contemporary illustrations; items of uniform, Black Watch Museum, Perth, Scotland.*
71. *Malibran; contemporary illustrations.*
72/73. *Knötel.*
74. *Olmes, after original lithographs.*
75. *Olmes, after original lithographs.*
76. *After Carl Vernet.*
77. *Hourtoulle.*
78. *Knötel, after contemporary illustrations.*
79. *Knötel, and 'Tradition' No. 38, after G. A. Embleton.*
80. *Olmes, after original lithograph.*

GLOSSARY

Aiguillette A loop of cord or lace attached to an epaulette.

Atiradores Sharpshooters of the Portuguese Caçadores.

'Barrelled', or 'Barrel' sash Cloth sash with loops or 'barrels' of a different colour.

Bicorn Cocked hat with two corners.

Brassard Cloth armband worn as a distinguishing feature.

Busby Fur cap, often with a cloth 'bag', favoured by hussars.

Caçadores Portuguese Light Infantry.

Chasseur Light Infantry.

Chasseur à Cheval Light Cavalry.

Colpack See 'Busby'.

Cuirass Breastplate (also applied to backplate) worn by heavy cavalry.

Czapka Polish-style, square-topped headdress, worn by Lancers.

Dolman Tailless braided jacket, as worn by hussars.

Epaulette Cloth or lace shoulder decoration, with a hanging fringe.

Facings The collar, cuffs, lapels and sometimes turnbacks of a uniform, often a different colour to the body of the coat.

Gorget Mark of officers' rank; a crescent-shaped metal ornament hung at the neck, a relic of medieval armour.

Grenadiers Elite infantry; term originally applied in the seventeenth and eighteenth centuries to troops armed with hand-grenades.

Hessian boots Boots with a 'V'-shaped cut at the front, often edged round the top with lace.

Hussar Light cavalry; the term originally Hungarian.

Jäger German term for riflemen.

Kiwer Russian pattern of shako adopted in 1812.

Kollet Prussian-style jacket.

Kurtka Polish-style jacket with 'plastron' lapels.

Kusket Swedish 'round hat' with fur crest.

Litewka Loose, frequently knee-length coat as worn by the Prussian Landwehr.

Mirliton Peakless shako with coloured cloth streamer, worn by hussars.

Pelisse Fur-edged jacket worn by hussars.

Pouch Small leather box worn on a belt, often containing cartridges.

Raupenhelm Leather-crested helmet worn by numerous German states, particularly Bavaria.

Sabretache Decorated leather case hung from sword-belt.

Schirmütze Cloth cap as worn by Prussian Landwehr.

Schützen   German term for sharpshooters.

Shabraque   Decorated horsecloth worn under the saddle.

Shoulderscale   Epaulette constructed of overlapping metal scales.

Supreveste   Cloth 'over-jacket' cut in the shape of a cuirass, worn by Russian and German royal bodyguards.

Tarleton   British-style light cavalry helmet, of leather with a fur crest.

Turnback   Turned-back section of the tail of a coat; frequently a different colour to the body of the coat.

Voltigeurs   French light infantry.

Wings   Crescent-shaped cloth epaulettes worn on the ends of the shoulder-straps.

APPENDIX

The Grande Armée 1812 – Order of Battle

Napoleon's Grande Armée which invaded Russia in 1812 contained more foreign than French regiments; it was the only occasion when so many European nations marched under a unified command. The large number of European states over which Napoleon had domination does much to explain the development and interchange of styles of military fashion during the period, the majority being clothed in uniforms of French design or inspiration.

The following list includes the names of Divisional commanders, and where necessary, the nationality is given after the regimental name.

HEADQUARTERS
Battalion de Neuchâtel (Swiss); 1 Btn.
Guides of the Chief (French); 1 Co.
Gendarmerie Imperiale (French); 1 Sqdn.

IMPERIAL GUARD – Bessierès and Mortier
1st Division (Delaborde)
    4th, 5th and 6th Tirailleurs of the Guard (French); 2 Btns. each
    4th, 5th and 6th Voltigeurs of the Guard (French); 2 Btns. each
2nd Division (Rouget)
    1st Voltigeurs of the Guard (French); 2 Btns.
    1st Tirailleurs of the Guard (French); 2 Btns.
    Fusilier-Chasseurs of the Guard (French); 2 Btns.
    Fusilier-Grenadiers of the Guard (French); 2 Btns.
    Flanquers of the Guard (French); 2 Btns.
3rd Division (Lefèvre)
    1st and 2nd Chasseurs of the Guard (French); 2 Btns. each
    1st and 2nd Grenadiers of the Guard (French); 2 Btns. each
    3rd Grenadiers of the Guard (Dutch); 2 Btns.
Cavalry of the Guard
    Grenadiers à Cheval of the Guard (French); 5 Sqdns.
    Chasseurs à Cheval of the Guard (French); 5 Sqdns.
    Mamelukes of the Guard; 1 Co.
    Dragoons of the Guard (French); 5 Sqdns.
    Elite Gendarmes of the Guard (French); 2 Sqdns.
    1st Lancers of the Guard (Polish); 4 Sqdns.
    2nd Lancers of the Guard (Dutch); 4 Sqdns.

Appendix

Attached to the Guard

 Portuguese Chasseurs à Cheval; 3 Sqdns.

 7th Chevau-Légers-Lanciers (Polish); 4 Sqdns.

 Velites du Prince Borghese (Italian); 1 Btn.

 Velites of the Tuscan Guard (Italian); 1 Btn.

 Spanish Engineers; 1 Btn.

Division Claparede

 1st, 2nd, 3rd and 4th Regiments, Vistula Legion (Polish); 3 Btns. each

FIRST ARMY CORPS – Davout

1st Division (Morand)

 17th and 30th Infantry (French); 5 Btns. each

 13th Light Infantry (French); 5 Btns.

2nd Division (Friant)

 15th Light Infantry (French); 5 Btns.

 33rd and 48th Infantry (French); 5 Btns. each

 Regiment Joseph Napoleon (Spanish); 2 Btns.

3rd Division (Gudin)

 7th Light Infantry (French); 5 Btns.

 12th and 21st Infantry (French); 5 Btns. each

 127th Infantry (French); 2 Btns.

 8th Confederation Regiment (Mecklenburg–Strelitz); 1 Btn.

4th Division (Dessaix)

 33rd Light Infantry (French); 4 Btns.

 85th and 108th Infantry (French); 5 Btns. each

5th Division (Compans)

 25th, 57th, 61st and 111th Infantry (French); 5 Btns. each

Corps Cavalry (Girardin)

 1st, 2nd and 3rd Chasseurs à Cheval (French); 4 Sqdns. each

 9th Lancers (Polish); 4 Sqdns.

SECOND ARMY CORPS – Oudinot

6th Division (Legrand)

 26th Light Infantry (French); 4 Btns.

 19th and 56th Infantry (French); 4 Btns. each

 128th Infantry (French); 2 Btns.

 3rd Portuguese Infantry; 2 Btns.

8th Division (Verdier)

 11th Light Infantry (French); 4 Btns.

 2nd Infantry (French); 5 Btns.

37th Infantry (French); 4 Btns.

124th Infantry (French); 3 Btns.

9th Division (Merle)

1st Swiss Infantry; 2 Btns.

2nd, 3rd and 4th Swiss Infantry; 3 Btns. each

123rd Infantry (French); 4 Btns.

3rd Provisional Regiment (Croatian); 2 Btns.

Corps Cavalry

7th, 20th, 23rd and 24th Chasseurs à Cheval (French); 4 Sqdns. each

8th Chevau-Légers-Lanciers (Polish); 4 Sqdns.

THIRD ARMY CORPS – Ney

10th Division (Ledru)

24th Light Infantry (French); 4 Btns.

46th and 72nd Infantry (French); 4 Btns. each

129th Infantry (French); 2 Btns.

1st Portuguese Infantry; 2 Btns.

11th Division (Razout)

4th, 18th and 93rd Infantry (French); 4 Btns. each

2nd Portuguese Infantry; 2 Btns.

Illyrian Regiment; 4 Btns.

25th Division (Marchand)

1st, 2nd, 4th, 6th and 7th Infantry (Württemberg); 2 Btns. each

1st and 2nd Jägers (Württemberg); 1 Btn. each

1st and 2nd Light Infantry (Württemberg); 1 Btn. each

Corps Cavalry (Wollwarth)

11th Hussars (French); 4 Sqdns.

6th Chevau-Légers-Lanciers (French); 3 Sqdns.

4th and 28th Chasseurs à Cheval (French); 4 Sqdns. each

Chevaulegers (Württemberg); 4 Sqdns.

Leib-Chevaulegers (Württemberg); 4 Sqdns.

3rd and 4th Mounted Jägers (Württemberg); 4 Sqdns. each

FOURTH ARMY CORPS – Eugène

Italian Guard (Lecchi)

Guards of Honour (Italian); 1 Co.

Royal Velites (Italian); 2 Btns.

Elite Regiment (Italian); 2 Btns.

Conscripts of the Guard (Italian); 2 Btns.

Dragoon Guards (Italian); 2 Sqdns.

Queen's Dragoons (Italian); 2 Sqdns.

13th Division (Delzons)

8th Light Infantry (French); 2 Btns.

84th, 92nd and 106th Infantry (French); 4 Btns. each

1st Provisional Regiment (Croatian); 2 Btns.

14th Division (Broussier)

18th Light Infantry (French); 2 Btns.

9th, 35th and 53rd Infantry (French); 4 Btns. each

Regiment Joseph Napoleon (Spanish); 2 Btns.

15th Division (Pino)

1st Light Infantry (Italian); 1 Btn.

3rd Light Infantry (Italian); 4 Btns.

2nd and 3rd Infantry (Italian); 4 Btns. each

Dalmatian Regiment (Italian); 3 Btns.

Corps Cavalry

9th and 19th Chasseurs à Cheval (French); 3 Sqdns. each

1st and 2nd Chasseurs à Cheval (Italian); 4 Sqdns. each

FIFTH ARMY CORPS – Poniatowski

16th Division (Zajonczek)

3rd, 13th, 15th and 16th Infantry (Polish); 3 Btns. each

17th Division (Dombrowski)

1st, 6th, 14th and 17th Infantry (Polish); 3 Btns. each

18th Division (Kamieniecki)

2nd, 8th and 12th Infantry (Polish); 3 Btns. each

Corps Cavalry (Kaminski)

1st, 4th and 5th Chasseurs à Cheval (Polish); 4 Sqdns. each

12th Lancers (Polish); 4 Sqdns.

13th Hussars (Polish); 4 Sqdns.

SIXTH ARMY CORPS – St. Cyr

19th Division (Deroy)

1st, 3rd and 6th Light Infantry (Bavarian); 1 Btn. each

1st, 4th, 8th, 9th and 10th Infantry (Bavarian); 2 Btns. each

20th Division (Wrede)

2nd, 4th and 5th Light Infantry (Bavarian); 1 Btn. each

2nd, 3rd, 5th, 6th, 7th and 11th Infantry (Bavarian); 2 Btns. each

Corps Cavalry

3rd, 4th, 5th and 6th Chevaulegers (Bavarian); 4 Sqdns. each

SEVENTH ARMY CORPS – Reynier

21st Division (Lecoq)
  Liebenau Grenadier Btn. (Saxon); 1 Btn.
  Regiment Prinz Clemens (Saxon); 2 Btns.
  Regiment Prince Friedrich August (Saxon); 2 Btns.
  Regiment Prince Anton (Saxon); 3 Btns.
  1st Light Infantry (Saxon); 1 Btn.

22nd Division (Gutschmidt)
  Grenadier Btn. von Anger (Saxon); 1 Btn.
  Grenadier Btn. von Spiegel (Saxon); 1 Btn.
  2nd Light Infantry (Saxon); 2 Btns.
  Regiment König (Saxon); 2 Btns.
  Regiment Niesemeuschel (Saxon); 2 Btns.
  Grenadier Battalion Eychelburg (Saxon); 1 Btn.

Corps Cavalry (Gablentz)
  Saxon Hussars; 8 Sqdns.
  Regiment Polenz (Saxon); 4 Sqdns.
  Regiment Prinz Clemens (Saxon); 4 Sqdns.

EIGHTH ARMY CORPS – Junot

23rd Division (Tharreau)
  2nd and 3rd Light Infantry (Westphalian); 1 Btn. each
  2nd, 3rd and 7th Infantry (Westphalian); 3 Btns. each
  6th Infantry (Westphalian); 2 Btns.

24th Division (Ochs)
  Elite Chasseur-Carabiniers (Westphalian); 1 Btn.
  Guard Chasseurs (Westphalian); 1 Btn.
  Guard Grenadiers (Westphalian); 1 Btn.
  1st Light Infantry (Westphalian); 1 Btn.
  5th Infantry (Westphalian); 2 Btns.

Corps Cavalry
  1st and 2nd Hussars (Westphalian); 4 Sqdns. each
  Garde du Corps (Westphalian); 1 Co.
  Guard Chevaulegers (Westphalian); 4 Sqdns.

NINTH ARMY CORPS – Victor

12th Division (Partouneaux)
  10th Light Infantry (French); 1 Btn.
  29th Light Infantry (French); 4 Btns.
  44th Infantry (French); 2 Btns.

125th Infantry (French); 3 Btns.

126th Infantry (French); 4 Btns.

Provisional Regiment (French); 3 Btns. (one battalion from each of the 36th, 51st and 55th Infantry)

26th Division (Daendels)

1st, 2nd and 4th Infantry (Berg); 2 Btns. each

3rd Infantry (Berg); 1 Btn.

1st, 2nd and 3rd Infantry (Baden); 2 Btns. each

Light Infantry (Baden); 1 Btn.

Leibgarde (Hesse–Darmstadt); 2 Btns.

Leib-Regiment (Hesse–Darmstadt); 2 Btns.

Garde Fusiliers (Hesse–Darmstadt); 2 Btns.

8th Infantry (Westphalian); 2 Btns.

28th Division (Girard)

4th, 7th and 9th Infantry (Polish); 3 Btns. each

Regiment von Low (Saxon); 2 Btns.

Regiment von Rechten (Saxon); 2 Btns.

Corps Cavalry (Fournier)

1st Lancers (Berg); 3 Sqdns.

Chevau Légers (Hesse–Darmstadt); 3 Sqdns.

Regiment Prince John (Saxon); 4 Sqdns.

Baden Hussars; 4 Sqdns.

TENTH ARMY CORPS – Macdonald

7th Division (Grandjean)

5th, 10th and 11th Infantry (Polish); 4 Btns. each

13th Infantry (Bavarian); 2 Btns.

1st Infantry (Westphalian); 2 Btns.

27th Division (York)

1st, 2nd, 3rd, 4th, 5th and 6th Combined Infantry (Prussian); 3 Btns. each

East Prussian Jägers; 1 Btn.

2nd East Prussian Fusiliers; 1 Btn.

Corps Cavalry

1st and 2nd Combined Hussars (Prussian); 4 Sqdns. each

1st and 2nd Combined Dragoons (Prussian); 4 Sqdns. each

ELEVENTH ARMY CORPS – Augerau

30th Division (Heudelet)

1st and 7th Provisional Regiments (French); 3 Btns. each

6th, 8th, 9th and 17th Provisional Regiments (French); 4 Btns. each

31st Division (LaGrange)
  10th and 12th Provisional Regiments (French); 3 Btns. each
  11th and 13th Provisional Regiments (French); 4 Btns. each
32nd Division (Durutte)
  Regiment de Belle Isle (French penal regiment); 3 Btns.
  Regiment de Walcheren (French penal regiment); 3 Btns.
  7th Confederation Regiment (Würzburg); 3 Btns.
  Würzburg Chevaulegers; 1 Sqdn.
  Regiment de Rhé (French penal regiment); 3 Btns.
  1st and 2nd Mediterranean Regiments (Italian); 3 Btns. each
33rd Division (Destrées)
  Marines and Velites (Neapolitan); 4 Btns.
  5th, 6th and 7th Infantry (Neapolitan); 2 Btns. each
  Guards of Honour and Velites (Neapolitan); 4 Sqdns.
34th Division (Morand)
  22nd Light Infantry (French); 2 Btns.
  3rd, 29th, 105th and 113th Infantry (French); 10 Btns. total
  3rd Confederation Regiment (Frankfurt); 3 Btns.
  4th Confederation Regiment (Saxony); 3 Btns.
  5th Confederation Regiment (Anhalt and Lippe); 2 Btns.
  6th Confederation Regiment (Schwarzburg, Waldeck and Reuss); 2 Btns.
  Regiment Prinz Maximilian (Saxon); 3 Btns.
  4th Infantry (Westphalian); 3 Btns.
  Dragoons (French); 1 Co. from each of 2nd, 5th, 12th, 13th, 14th, 17th, 19th and 20th Regts.; 4 Sqdns.

FIRST CAVALRY CORPS – Nansouty
1st Light Cavalry Division (Bruyers)
  7th and 8th Hussars (French); 4 Sqdns. each
  9th Chevau-Légers-Lanciers (French); 4 Sqdns.
  16th Chasseurs à Cheval (French); 4 Sqdns.
  6th and 8th Lancers (Polish); 4 Sqdns.
  2nd Combined Hussars (Prussian); 4 Sqdns.
1st Heavy Cavalry Division (St. Germain)
  2nd, 3rd and 9th Cuirassiers (French); 4 Sqdns. each
  1st Chevau-Légers-Lanciers (French); 3 Sqdns.
5th Heavy Cavalry Division (Valence)
  6th, 11th and 12th Cuirassiers (French); 4 Sqdns. each
  5th Chevau-Légers-Lanciers (French); 3 Sqdns.

SECOND CAVALRY CORPS – Montbrun

2nd Light Cavalry Division (Sebastiani)
   11th and 12th Chasseurs à Cheval (French); 4 Sqdns. each
   5th and 9th Hussars (French); 4 Sqdns. each
   10th Hussars (Polish); 3 Sqdns.
   Combined Lancers (Prussian); 4 Sqdns.

2nd Heavy Cavalry Division (Wathiez)
   5th, 8th and 10th Cuirassiers (French); 4 Sqdns. each
   2nd Chevau-Légers-Lanciers (French); 3 Sqdns.

4th Heavy Cavalry Division (Defrance)
   1st and 2nd Carabiniers (French); 4 Sqdns. each
   1st Cuirassiers (French); 4 Sqdns.
   4th Chevau-Légers-Lanciers (French); 3 Sqdns.

THIRD CAVALRY CORPS – Grouchy

3rd Light Cavalry Division (Castel)
   8th, 6th and 25th Chasseurs à Cheval (French); 4 Sqdns. each
   6th Hussars (French); 4 Sqdns.
   1st and 2nd Chevaulegers (Bavarian); 4 Sqdns. each
   Regiment Prince Albert (Saxon); 4 Sqdns.

3rd Heavy Cavalry Division (Doumerc)
   4th, 7th and 14th Cuirassiers (French); 4 Sqdns. each
   3rd Chevau-Légers-Lanciers (French); 3 Sqdns.

6th Heavy Cavalry Division (Lahoussaye)
   7th, 23rd, 28th and 30th Dragoons (French); 3 Sqdns. each

FOURTH CAVALRY CORPS – Latour-Maubourg

4th Light Cavalry Division (Rozniecki)
   2nd, 3rd, 7th, 11th, 15th and 16th Lancers (Polish); 3 Sqdns. each

7th Heavy Cavalry Division (Lorge)
   Garde du Corps (Saxon); 4 Sqdns.
   Zastrow Cuirassiers (Saxon); 4 Sqdns.
   14th Cuirassiers (Polish); 2 Sqdns.
   1st and 2nd Cuirassiers (Westphalian); 4 Sqdns. each

AUSTRIAN AUXILIARY CORPS – Schwarzenberg

Cavalry Division Frimont
   Hohenzollern and O'Reilly Dragoons (Austrian); 8 Sqdns. each
   Erzherzog Dragoons (Austrian); 6 Sqdns.
   Kaiser, Hessen–Homburg, Blankenstein and Kienmayer Hussars (Austrian);
     8 Sqdns. each

Division Bianchi
    Regiments Hiller, Colloredo–Mansfeld, Simbchen and Alvinzy (Austrian);
        2 Btns. each
    Grenadier Btns. Kirchenbetter and Brezinski (Austrian); 1 Btn. each
Division Siegenthal
    Regiments Prinz de Ligne, Czartoryski, Davidovich and Sattulinski (Austrian);
        2 Btns. each
    7th Jägers (Austrian); 1 Btn.
    Warasdiner Border Infantry (Austrian); 2 Btns.
Division Trautenberg
    Regiment von Würtzburg (Austrian); 4 Btns.
    5th Jägers (Austrian); 1 Btn.
    Sankt Georger Border Infantry (Austrian); 2 Btns.

Even those regiments officially 'French' often contained foreigners, and some were wholly foreign; for example, the 111th Infantry (Piedmontese), 113th Infantry (Tuscan), 123rd to 126th Infantry (Dutch), 11th Light Infantry (Swiss and Piedmontese), 33rd Light Infantry (Dutch), 14th Cuirassiers and 11th Hussars (Dutch), 8th Chevau-Légers-Lanciers (Polish), 9th Chevau-Légers-Lanciers (German), 19th Chasseurs à Cheval (Swiss), 28th Chasseurs à Cheval (Tuscan).

LIST OF UNIFORMS BY NATIONALITY

	Date	Plate No.
Nassau		
Jägers	1807	13
Poland (see also *Warsaw*)		
Artillery	1799–1808	4
General Officers	1796	59
1st Polish Light Horse of the Imperial Guard		
(French service)	1811	53
Portugal		
Caçadores	1808	30
Portuguese Legion (French service)	1809	35
Prussia		
10th Colberg Regiment	1812	69
General Staff	1808–1812	31
Garde Jäger Battalion	1809	38
Landwehr Infantry	1814	79
2nd Life Hussars	1809	29
Russia		
Chevaliers Garde	1796	2
Cuirassiers	1812	72/73
Infantry	1812	74
Jägers	1809	34
Light Infantry	1814	80
Saxe–Coburg–Saalfeld		
Infantry	1809	33
Saxony		
Chevau-Légers	1812	60
Garde du Corps	1812	77
Guard Grenadiers	1806	18
Jäger Corps	1813	52
Kurfürst Cuirassier Regiment	1803	5
Light Infantry	1810	52
Surgeon	1810	46

List of Uniforms by Nationality

	Date	Plate No.
Spain		
Guerrillas	1809	26
7th Lancers	1811	54
Villaviciosa Dragoons	1806	17
Sweden		
Grenadier Corps of the Life Brigade	1813	22
Life Grenadier Regiment	1813	22
Life Guard	1807	20
Switzerland		
Légion Sainte-Galloise	1810	45
Light Cavalry	1800	3
Neuchâtel Battalion (French service)	1812	56/57
4th Swiss Regiment (French service)	1812	76
Valaison Battalion (French service)	1810	55
Volunteer Jägers of Zürich	1805	10
Warsaw (Grand Duchy)		
Horse Artillery	1808	4
The Krakus	1812	65
Vistula Legion (French service)	1810	48
Westphalia		
Garde du Corps	1810	44
Württemburg		
Artillery	1812	75
Guard Jägers	1808	28

LIST OF UNIFORMS BY ARM OF SERVICE

Artillery	Bavaria	68
	France	56/57
	Poland	4
	Switzerland	45
	Württemburg	75
Cuirassiers	France	11
	Russia	72/73
	Saxony	5
Dragoons	France	19
	Spain	17
Engineers	France	36, 47, 56/57
General Staff	France	8/9, 71
	Great Britain	40/41
	Poland	59
	Prussia	31
Grenadiers	Austria	32, 39
	Bavaria	37
	Cleve–Berg	67
	France	55, 64
	Prussia	69
	Saxony	18
	Sweden	22
	Switzerland	45
Guard Regiments	France	16, 27, 47, 50, 53, 64
	Italy	23, 24/25
	Prussia	38
	Russia	2
	Saxony	18, 77
	Sweden	20
	Westphalia	44
	Württemburg	28

Hussars	Baden	12
	France	1, 7
	Great Britain	6, 61
	Prussia	29
Infantry	Austria	32, 39
	Bavaria	37
	Brunswick	42
	Cleve–Berg	67
	Denmark	21
	France	14, 35, 48, 55, 62, 64, 66, 76
	Great Britain	6, 40/41, 51, 70
	Hanover	78
	Holland	15
	Portugal	30
	Prussia	38, 69, 79
	Russia	34, 74, 80
	Saxe–Coburg–Saalfeld	33
	Saxony	18, 52
	Spain	26
	Sweden	22
	Switzerland	10, 45
Jägers	Brunswick	42
	Denmark	21
	Hanover	78
	Portugal	30
	Prussia	38
	Russia	34, 80
	Saxony	52
	Switzerland	10
Light Cavalry	Baden	12
	France	1, 7, 16, 27, 35, 43, 50, 53, 58, 63
	Great Britain	6, 61
	Hesse–Darmstadt	49
	Nassau	13
	Prussia	29

	Saxony	60
	Spain	54
	Switzerland	3
	Warsaw	65
Light Infantry	France	62
	Great Britain	40/41, 51
	Holland	15
	Russia	80
	Saxony	52
Medical Staff	Bavaria	46
	Saxony	46